Rain
Gardens

SUSTAINABLE LANDSCAPING
FOR A BEAUTIFUL YARD AND A HEALTHY WORLD

By Lynn M. Steiner and Robert W. Domm

Voyageur Press

CONTENTS

AN INTRODUCTION TO RAIN GARDENS

We live in a world of sunlight and water where,

balanced between the cycles of night and day, of

flood and drought, and the changing of the seasons,

life flourishes. One of the most important cycles

of nature is the movement of water. Water moves

through the atmosphere, through and across the

earth, and through every living thing. Without water

there is no life. With water, even on planets other than

our own, life is possible.

Water is constantly on the move, flowing over and under Earth's surface,
moving through the air, and nourishing every living thing.

The movement of water is not random. Water is continuously cycling through the environment: falling as rain, evaporating into clouds, and passing through every living thing. This cycling and recycling of water through Earth's biosphere is called the water cycle, and it works the same way in the tropics of Florida, the rainforests of Washington State, and the prairies of Minnesota.

Water Everywhere

Water saturates the earth and covers three quarters of its surface. Clouds of water vapor swirl through the atmosphere, and vast quantities of water lie in hidden reserves deep underground. The volume of water on earth is so enormous that it is measured in cubic miles of water (imagine a cube one mile wide, one mile long, and one mile high).

By far the majority of the earth's water, about 321 million cubic miles worth, lies in the oceans, seas, and salty bays. About 22,000 cubic miles of water is stored in Earth's freshwater lakes and rivers and another 5.8 million cubic miles of water lies underground in the earth's aquifers. The plants and animals of Earth (including humans) hold another 269 million cubic miles of water.

Water vapor in the air totals 3,100 cubic miles, and each day, 4 cubic miles of that total falls as rain or snow on the lower forty-eight states. Although only a small percentage of the total rain and snow that falls each day falls on urban areas, the pollutants, sediment, and other problems generated by runoff from towns and cities impacts vast areas downstream.

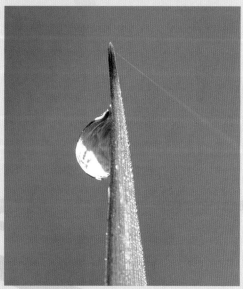

ABOVE LEFT: Water on Earth is stored as surface water (lakes, rivers, or oceans), as groundwater, and in the atmosphere.

LEFT: Plants expel excess water through their leaves and into the atmosphere in a process called transpiration.

The Water Cycle

The water cycle refers simply to how water moves through the environment. The earth contains the same amount of water as it did when it formed 4.5 billion years ago, and the only thing that changes is whether the water exists as liquid water, solid ice, or water vapor.

As the sun heats and cools the earth, water changes from one state to another. Cold weather turns water to ice, ice melts back into liquid water, evaporation turns liquid water to vapor, and when the air becomes saturated with water vapor, it falls to Earth as rain or snow.

Water held in freshwater lakes and rivers provides most of the world's drinking water. When lakes and rivers become polluted by storm water runoff, the world's clean drinking water is jeopardized.

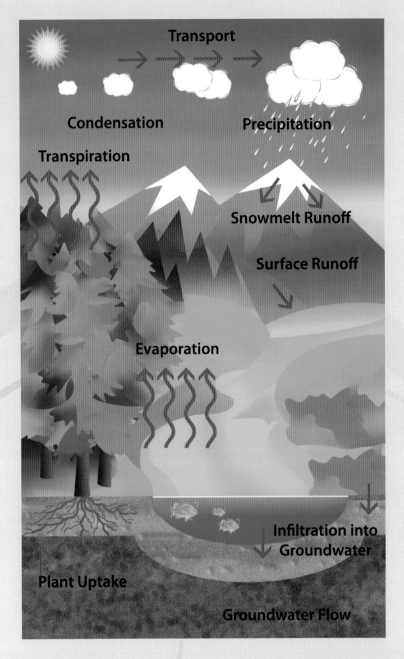

The water cycle shows how water moves over and through the earth and its atmosphere. © *Jeffrey C. Domm*

A well-designed rain garden is an attractive way to capture storm water and keep it on site.

Right as Rain: Why We Should Care about Storm Water

The easiest part of the water cycle to observe is rainfall. The amount of rain that falls determines what types of plants and animals thrive in a region and which ones don't. In the past it also influenced where people could or couldn't live. Nowadays, that has changed. Technology has even brought water to the desert and, along with it, plenty of people.

The growth of large cities has caused a glitch in the natural water cycle. The roofs, roads, and parking lots of cities and towns have replaced natural surfaces, such as grasslands, forests, and farmland. These urban surfaces absorb very little rainfall. Instead, the water runs off.

In a typical forest or grassland, most rainwater is absorbed into the ground where it is taken up by plants or stored as groundwater. Not so in most cities. Very little of the rain that falls in a city is absorbed into the ground. Instead, the rainwater washes pollutants and trash from streets and parking lots into the storm drain and deposits it, without treatment, into a nearby lake or river. This is an efficient way to prevent flooded streets, but it also causes many problems.

When the rain from a downpour moves into the storm drain it gains speed and energy. By the time it empties into a local lake or river, the clean water from a rainstorm has become a fast-moving deluge of dirty water. This surge of tainted water wreaks havoc on fish and other water-dwelling creatures, clogging their gills with silt and sweeping smaller animals downstream. Storm water runoff causes erosion of stream banks, damaging property and washing tons of soil into the water.

Fertilizers and other lawn chemicals are also part of this toxic soup. Over-applied fertilizer that has been washed into the drain during a rainstorm is an enormous problem in urban waterways. The active ingredients of lawn fertilizer, nitrogen and phosphorus, are normally scarce in lakes and rivers; this helps hold down aquatic plant growth. When these two chemicals become abundant, plant growth explodes and water quality suffers. Excessive plant growth raises the temperature of water, and when the plants die and decay, it robs the water of oxygen. High water temperature and low oxygen levels spell disaster for fish and the small creatures they rely on for food.

No one goes out during a rainstorm and watches the runoff pouring from a drain pipe into a river, and people rarely link dirty water, eroded stream banks, and lifeless streams to storm water runoff. The unfortunate truth is that urban runoff is a huge water quality problem. The good news is that you can do something about it.

ABOVE LEFT:
Rain falling on
vegetated areas is
quickly absorbed,
while rain that falls on
roads, parking lots, or
rooftops runs off.

ABOVE RIGHT:
Rain that runs off
roadways is often
collected in catch
basins and directed
to local streams
and rivers without
treatment of any kind.

LEFT: Bumblebees are
important pollinators
in a rain garden
(landing on
Monarda fistulosa).

Land Use and Runoff

As the use of the land changes, so does its ability to absorb and recycle rainwater. In well-established woodlands and grasslands, very little water runs off the land during a typical rainstorm. There are several reasons for this. First, heavy vegetation slows rainwater down before and after it has hit the ground, allowing it more time to absorb into the earth. Second, the ground in a typical woodland or grassland is not compacted by human activity, so it more readily absorbs water. Also, the root systems of plants not only take up water quickly but, with the help of animals and insects, keep the soil loose and full of small spaces where water can be stored.

There are, of course, still times when natural areas flood. Periodic flooding is a natural occurrence that serves a necessary ecological function. But the flush of water that is collected by a storm drain after a rainstorm bypasses the natural process that slows the water and gives it time to absorb into the ground. This glitch in the water cycle can cause flash flooding, wash sediment and trash into rivers, and stress or kill aquatic animals.

Rain that falls on natural landscapes replenishes surface water, nourishes plants, and recharges the aquifer.

Urban rainwater runoff carries pollutants, trash, and sediment into waterways.

The "Only Rain in the Drain" drain stenciling campaign promotes storm water runoff awareness.

Only Rain in the Drain

Did you know that the rain collected in the storm drain goes directly to local lakes, rivers, and streams without treatment of any kind?

When pet waste, yard clippings, motor oil, or trash are put in the storm drain, it is the same as putting it directly in our waterways. Even washing your car in a street or driveway that drains to a catch basin pollutes lakes and rivers. Never dump anything into a catch basin or storm drain that you don't want to see in the local lake or river. Always wash your car at a commercial car wash or on a grassy area where the soap and road grime can be absorbed into the soil.

A nationwide campaign is under way to educate people about the adverse effects of dumping materials into storm drains. Look for the slogan "Only Rain in the Drain" or "No Dumping, Drains to River" stenciled on or around catch basins and remember to educate your neighbors about the harmful effects of dumping waste into the storm drain.

Storm water discharge into public waterways is strictly regulated by the EPA.

Storm Water Permitting

As part of the Clean Water Act, Congress instituted the National Pollution Discharge Elimination System (NPDES) permitting process. Scientists had long realized that water being discharged into America's waterways contained a witch's brew of pollutants. The NPDES permitting process sought to improve water quality by reducing these pollutants.

Prior to NPDES permitting, only one third of our nation's waters were safe for fishing and swimming, and American farms lost 2.25 billion tons of soil each year to runoff. The nitrogen and phosphorus from fertilizer poured into our rivers creating thick mats of oxygen-depleting vegetation.

With NPDES permitting now firmly in place, water quality has improved dramatically. Now it is safe to fish and swim in two-thirds of America's waterways, and agricultural erosion has been reduced by one billion tons annually.

Among other measures, the NPDES permit process calls for controls on point source discharges that include ditches or pipes that discharge pollutants into public waterways. Point source discharges come from municipal storm sewers, storm pipes from maintenance garages, school grounds, private manufacturing facilities, or even from private homes.

If your neighborhood has a storm drain or sewer that collects rainwater from roadways and private property, chances are your town or county owns and operates the system. These Municipal Separate Storm Sewer Systems (or MS4s) most likely operate under NPDES permits that set down rules to lessen the negative effects of storm water runoff.

To comply with these rules, many communities encourage residents to control runoff at its source by installing rain gardens, rain barrels, or riparian buffer zones, even offering incentives to home and business owners who install runoff control devices. Check with your local government to see if your rain garden or rain barrel qualifies for an incentive.

The Watershed Approach

To better understand and relate how water moves through the environment, scientists and land use planners often think in terms of watersheds. A watershed is the total land area that drains to a particular river or other water body. Everyone, no matter where they live, lives in a watershed.

Watershed boundaries are set by the geography of the land and can vary greatly in size from a few to many thousands of square miles. Often, a large watershed is broken down into smaller sub-watersheds. This helps planners to better understand the dynamics of the larger system and to pinpoint water quality problem areas.

Pollution in the upper reaches of a watershed can have a profound impact on areas downstream. Improving storm water runoff quality in the upstream reaches of a watershed improves downstream water quality.

Scientists and planners use the watershed model to better address water pollution problems.

Wild bergamot (*Monarda fistulosa*)

What Is a Rain Garden?

A rain garden is a plant bed that collects rain runoff from your roof, driveway, patio, or other waterproof outdoor surface. A pipe connected to a downspout or an above-ground channel conveys the water to the garden. In a rain garden, the excess water is absorbed quickly into the soil.

At first glance, a rain garden differs very little from any other flowerbed. Look closer to see that a rain garden is built in a shallow depression, usually about six to eight inches deep. The slight depression allows the garden to hold water for a short period of time while it is absorbed into the soil. The down-slope side of a garden built on an incline will also have a low earthen berm to help the garden hold the collected water.

A rain garden is not a pond or a wetland. Instead, it holds standing water for a very short time, usually less than twenty-four hours. This is true even after a heavy downpour.

It is the ability of a rain garden to absorb excess water that sets it apart from an ordinary garden. If the native soil in your yard does not absorb water quickly enough, then it must be re-worked to increase its water-absorbing ability before a rain garden is installed. Working a combination of sand and compost into the soil usually does the trick (see Chapter 1 for more information).

A positive difference between a rain garden and more traditional gardens is the amount of care a rain garden requires. Many traditional gardens, especially those that contain non-native varieties of plants, require an annual dose of fertilizer and pesticide to maintain a healthy planting. A rain garden planted with species that are native to your geographic region should never require fertilizer or pesticides to thrive.

Most rain gardens have a low berm on the down-slope side to help the garden retain runoff until it can be absorbed into the ground. © *Ward Wilson*

Why a Rain Garden?

Just as they should, storm drains remove excess rainwater quickly and efficiently from our roads and from around our homes. While the system is effective, it causes many difficulties as well. There are new green technologies being developed and put into practice every day to help solve this dilemma. Unfortunately, no single technology will make everything right. Instead, homeowners, developers, and city planners must take many small steps toward a practical solution.

One step you can take toward cleaner water is installing a rain garden. A rain garden combines the benefits of reducing storm water runoff with the appeal of a garden. Rain gardens cost very little to build, can be installed on just about any property, and provide a huge ecological benefit, all while adding to the beauty of your yard.

Rain gardens are designed to allow rainwater to follow the natural course of the water cycle (absorbed into the ground, taken up by plants, and evaporated back into the atmosphere). Rain gardens allow the rain that falls on your property to stay on your property where it recharges the groundwater and irrigates your trees and shrubs.

A rain garden in Louisville, Kentucky, collects runoff from two neighboring houses. © Ward Wilson

A rain garden doesn't have to be large to improve water quality.

A Beautiful Solution

Not only is a rain garden a beautiful solution to the negative effects of storm water runoff, it also is a welcome home to a large variety of wildlife. A manicured lawn provides little food or shelter for local birds and beneficial insects. In many cases, a lawn can seem devoid of life while a nearby rain garden in full summer bloom is alive with colorful birds, butterflies, and honey bees.

Rain gardens are home to predatory insects that eat the harmful bugs that are normally controlled by expensive and dangerous chemical pesticides.

Want to save money on your water bill? Then a rain garden is for you. Unlike a normal flower garden, rain gardens make good use of water that would have normally run off your property and into the storm drain. With the cost of water rising nearly everywhere and the reality of water rationing in many places, rain gardens make good economic sense.

Reducing water pollution is a goal we can all appreciate. Now, you can be part of the solution. By installing a rain garden, you reduce pollution, save water, and create a beautiful and useful habitat for creatures of all sorts. Now that's a win-win situation!

CHAPTER
1

PLANNING YOUR RAIN GARDEN

Planning a rain garden is as easy as planning any type

of garden. Elements common to all gardens, such as

what type of plants to include, the garden's size and

location, and ease of maintenance, all apply when

planning your rain garden. The main difference

in planning a rain garden is that its size and location

is dependent on how much rainwater runoff

you plan to collect and what impervious surfaces

you choose to collect from.

With a few exceptions, planning a rain garden is very similar to planning any other type of garden. © Paul Markert

Locating Your Garden

Your rain garden's function is to capture rainwater that was destined to run off your property. Instead of sending rain runoff to the local storm sewer, a rain garden temporarily stores the water and allows it to soak into the ground, watering your plants and recharging the local aquifer. Make certain that your rain garden serves its function as a beautiful space that cleanses rainwater and waters your plants by planning its location carefully.

A typical flower or vegetable garden requires frequent irrigation, so it can be located anywhere in your yard that is within reach of the garden hose. An established rain garden is irrigated by rainwater, so it must be close to a downspout or near another source of rainwater runoff, such as a driveway or walkway. As we will see, there are several ways to direct rainwater to your garden, so it is not necessary to locate the garden directly adjacent to the source of rainwater runoff.

Bear in mind the basics of maintenance when planning your garden's location. Make certain the area is accessible to any power equipment you plan to use both for the garden's construction and its future maintenance. Visualize what the garden will look like when it is mature, making certain that the plants will not outgrow the garden or that they will not intrude into other spaces in your yard or your neighbor's yard. A garden that is crowded into a corner or against a fence may be difficult to access for weeding or pruning, so keep the area around the garden open. Remember that small tree near your planned garden may throw little shade on the spot now, but it may dramatically change the sunlight characteristics of the site in just a few years.

RIGHT: Water from a downspout can be directed to a rain garden using a length of buried corrugated plastic pipe.

This rain garden is sited to capture runoff from a downspout and a patio.
© Connie Taillon

A vegetated swale.

Low Areas

It would seem logical to put a rain garden in a low area in the yard where water collects anyway. This might be a good choice, but it may require the most time, effort, and money to build such a garden. A low spot that holds water does so because the soil there does not drain well. This usually means that the soil is predominately clay or, if you live in certain areas, water collects there because it is trapped by bedrock or some other impervious geological feature.

In order to function properly, a rain garden must be well drained. If it is not, the garden will store the extra water that is directed to it from your roof or driveway. The purpose of creating a rain garden is not to make a water-logged quagmire. Instead, a rain garden should be well drained so that excess water pools for less than twenty-four hours before it is completely absorbed into the soil. Moreover, water-saturated soil will support only a few types of plants that are specifically adapted to that type of environment, and standing water creates a breeding ground for mosquitoes.

Rain garden plants provide a staging area for hunting insects like this dragonfly.

Careful thought should be given to placement of a rain garden to ensure it functions properly.

Locating a rain garden in a poorly drained area also means that the garden must be significantly larger than one located in a well drained area so that it can handle the excess water directed to it without flooding or becoming saturated. The better solution for building a rain garden in a poorly drained area is to replace the existing soil with a mix of sand, topsoil, and compost (see soil texture section on page 39). This, however, requires that the existing soil be removed and disposed of (at an extra effort and cost), and that some type of drainage system be installed to remove excess water that may percolate through the topsoil and become trapped by impervious soil under the garden.

If, on the other hand, an area of your yard collects water after a rainstorm but the water is then quickly absorbed into the ground, this may be an ideal place for your rain garden. Such an area will require only nominal site preparation and soil amendment to properly function. A soil test (see page 37) will still be needed to ensure your planting will not suffer from any soil deficiencies and ensure the area is large enough to accommodate any runoff directed to it.

A bed of sun-loving native plants makes a colorful and easily maintained alternative to mown grass in a roadside swale rain garden.

Working with an Existing Drainage Swale

Many neighborhoods have a system of grass swales that collect and remove rainwater from roadways and yards. A properly constructed swale is a gently sloping depression that conveys water slowly and completely downstream without creating a torrent after a large storm. Much like a rain garden, a well-functioning swale does not store excess water for long periods of time. If you have a grass swale that collects the runoff from your yard, the adjacent roadway, and a small amount of water from upstream, it may be a perfect place for a rain garden. Chapter 2 discusses how to convert an existing grass swale into a rain garden.

Swamp milkweed (*Asclepias incarnate*), yarrow (*Achillea*), and bee balm (*Monarda didyma*) are all good choices for rain gardens.

Rain gardens provide habitat for many interesting creatures, including this firefly.

Working around Existing Features

If your house has a septic tank and drain field for sanitary waste, place the rain garden well away from either structure. As they grow, the long roots that are common to many rain garden plants can clog drain fields and lateral lines. Even if you are connected to a municipal sanitary collection system, it is best to avoid planting your garden above your lateral line for the same reasons. If you don't know where your lateral line is located, your city engineer's office may be able to help you locate it or, if you have the blueprints for your home, the location of your sanitary lead should be shown on them.

When locating a rain garden in your yard, keep in mind existing features, such as large trees, fences, overhead wires (if you plan to plant a tree in your garden), and public utility structures that may require periodic inspection or maintenance. Before you begin any excavation, be sure to contact your local one-call utility notification hotline (8-1-1) to have any underground utilities on your property flagged (see sidebar).

Properly landscaped ground around a building always directs water away from the structure and never allows water to pool or collect near the foundation. Installing a rain garden adjacent to a building's foundation may lead to leaks in the basement or encourage rot in wooden floor joists or supports. To be safe, keep your rain garden at least ten feet from a building's foundation.

Call 8-1-1

To prevent accidental disturbance of buried public utilities when you are constructing your rain garden, make certain to call your state's one-call utility notification hotline. The hotline works with member utilities such as gas, electric, telephone, and cable providers to mark out the location of buried utility lines for contractors and homeowners before they begin a construction project. Dial 8-1-1 on your telephone a couple of days prior to beginning your project, and you will be routed to your local one-call center. After you contact your local one-call center, a representative will come to your property and flag all the underground utilities. There is no charge for the 8-1-1 service.

Be sure to contact your state's one-call utility hotline (8-1-1) before you dig. Workers will mark any underground utilities on your property.

Keep It Level

To avoid a large-scale excavation when installing your garden, choose a spot in your yard that is level or just slightly sloped. To be efficient, a rain garden must be level. If the garden is sloped downhill from where the water enters, water will collect in the rear of the garden and the garden's absorption efficiency will suffer. Also, if the garden is not level, water flow will redistribute mulch and soil to the lower end of the garden. A general rule is that if a location has a slope greater than twelve degrees, it is best to choose a different location because of the extra effort involved in creating a level garden.

A properly constructed rain garden will form a shallow depression or bowl where water can collect. The percent slope of the area you choose for your rain garden will determine the optimal depth of your garden's depression. If the slope is less than 5 percent, the garden need only be between three and five inches deep. A slope between 5 and 7 percent means the garden should be six to seven inches deep, and if the slope is between 8 and 12 percent, the garden should be about eight inches deep to best capture the rainwater after a storm.

Calculating Slope

To calculate the percent slope of the area you choose for your rain garden, you will need several simple tools and supplies: approximately fifty feet of heavy string, two stakes, a hammer, a string level, a tape measure, and a helper. Drive the first stake into the ground at the uphill end of your proposed garden and the second stake at the lower end and measure the distance between the stakes. Securely tie the end of the string to the uphill stake at the point where the stake enters the ground and stretch it to the downhill stake. Place the string level on the string halfway between the two stakes. Take up the slack in the string and raise or lower it until the string is level. When the string is level, have your helper measure the distance from the string to the ground on the downhill side of the setup. The percent slope is equal to the height of the level string at the downhill stake divided by the distance between the two stakes times 100. Be sure to use the same units (inches, feet, or meters) for both the height and distance.

ABOVE LEFT: Measuring and calculating the slope of the area you choose for your rain garden can be done quickly with a few simple items. The slope value will tell you if the spot is suitable for a rain garden.

LEFT: A string level is used to calculate slope.

A garden deeper than eight inches may present a trip-and-fall hazard and may look less like a garden and more like a crater in your lawn that is filled with plants.

If the garden is built on sloped ground, the bottom of the garden, or the bottom of the excavation, must also be level. This insures that water will infiltrate evenly into the ground under the garden's soil and avoid pockets of boggy soil. Gardens built on a severe slope will need a large earthen berm on the down-slope side to hold water in the garden until it can be absorbed. See Chapter 2 for more information on berms.

Building a garden on sloped ground also means that a large amount of soil must be excavated from the upslope end of the garden and/or soil must be added to the down-slope side to make the garden level. On gently sloping ground, the digging and soil redistribution will be minimal, but as the slope increases, so does the amount of work to make things level.

Planting a variety of flowering plants and grasses makes a rain garden visually appealing.

Lansing, Michigan's capital, has joined many other cities and enhanced their downtown streetscape with rain gardens.

Ordinance and Setback

Many communities have zoning ordinances that may restrict lawn usage or require a minimum setback from sidewalks, roads, property lines, etc. for gardens or other landscape projects on your property.

Private developments may also have rules or covenants that restrict the type and size of certain landscape features. If you are in doubt about your rain garden project, it is best to check out the rules first before any construction begins. If you approach skeptical officials with a detailed, well-thought-out plan for a rain garden and are prepared to explain the garden's benefits, it is usually easier to convince them to give the go-ahead or grant a variance for your project.

Low Impact Development

Low impact development (LID) is a comprehensive, on-site rainwater management approach. By filtering and storing rainwater on site, an LID site mimics predevelopment conditions. This approach is less expensive than building costly downstream storm water structures. This versatile approach to water management works equally well on new development, urban retrofits, and redevelopment sites.

LID techniques include the use of rain gardens, green roofs, porous parking areas and sidewalks, rain barrels, and open space to eliminate runoff at its source. In addition to these storm water structures, LID also seeks to reduce the reliance on pipes, ponds, and street-side curb and gutter to control storm water. Instead, LID focuses on providing buffer zones, drainage courses, groundwater recharge areas, and grading strategies to reduce runoff.

The traditional approach to storm water control design has been to build the system to handle a specific rainfall event, such as a one-hundred-year flood or a twenty-five-year storm. While these systems may perform well during their design event, they often over-perform during lower intensity events. By using a variety of controls designed to handle smaller storms that occur more frequently (e.g., weekly or monthly), LID practices mimic natural systems that can handle the high frequency, low rainfall events as well as the larger storms.

As with any new feature or idea, creating a positive public view is essential to success. If LID is a cost-effective alternative to traditional storm water management, and if it increases property value, then it is likely to be incorporated into building projects. LID has many other benefits in addition to cleaner water, including increased property values, greater flexibility for redevelopment, improved wildlife habitat, flooding and smog reduction, and energy savings.

With limited government funds available to expand or repair storm water infrastructure and the high cost of adding new downstream storm water controls, LID makes good economic sense for local governments, developers, and homeowners.

Rainwater from the roof is directed into a storage cistern at the visitor center of Bernheim Forest in Kentucky.

Rainwater runoff helps keep a koi pond filled at the visitor center of Bernheim Forest in Kentucky.

A green roof in early spring at the Bernheim Forest Visitor Center in Kentucky.

Green Roofs

Green roofs are a new application for an ancient practice. Once used out of necessity by people inhabiting grasslands with no other available building material, roofing made of living earth and plants now offers a way to reduce storm water runoff and enhance a building's energy efficiency. A simple green roof with only three inches of soil can reduce rainwater runoff by 50 percent compared to a traditional impervious roof—all while providing an extra layer of insulation against the heat and cold.

Green roofs consist of a layer of soil media covered with vegetation. Instead of rushing down a downspout and into a storm drain, rainwater that falls on a green roof follows a more natural course of uptake and transpiration by the roof's plants just as it does in a rain garden. Excess water from a heavy downpour still runs off a green roof, but slowly and after filtering through the soil media. A rain barrel or cistern used in tandem with a green roof can bring the storm runoff from a building to near zero.

Water-soaked soil media can add a lot of extra weight to a roof, and ordinary wood frame and unreinforced masonry buildings usually cannot withstand the extra weight. A qualified professional should assess the structural strength of a building before adding a green roof.

Green roofs have become a popular option for new construction projects that are environmentally friendly and energy efficient. Turning an existing, traditional roof into a green roof is certainly possible, and many people choose this route. Flat roofs work best, but by using a system of stabilization panels and mesh, a green roof can be installed on roofs with up to a thirty-degree slope. An under drain system or drainage layer is installed to channel excess water off the roof, and a root barrier and waterproof membrane protects the roof structure from damage.

Choose hardy plants like sedum and drought-resistant grasses for a green roof. Avoid plants with long roots to minimize damage to root barriers and waterproofing membranes. Avoid planting shrubs and trees for obvious reasons.

Rain gardens store snow during winter months and absorb the spring meltwater.

Planning for Winter

If you live in a part of the country that receives accumulating snow each winter, keep snow removal in mind when locating your garden. Rain gardens are an excellent place to store excess snow during the winter months. Not only does the melting snow get a chance to percolate back into the ground each spring, but the snow itself acts as an insulating blanket, protecting the roots of over-wintering plants from the dry winter air.

If your garden drains a road or walkway that is salted during the winter months, be aware that salt can accumulate in the garden's soil and adversely affect the health of many plants. Some plants tolerate high soil salt content better than others. If your garden is subjected to an annual influx of road salt, it may be wise to plant salt-tolerant grasses or forbs near the garden's inlet.

Goldfinch on winter seed head of purple coneflower (*Echinacea purpurea*).

LEFT: A full-sun rain garden in bloom can add a riot of color to any landscape.© *Connie Taillon*

ABOVE: A shady spot under the canopy of a mature tree is perfect for a rain garden filled with shade-loving plants. © *Connie Taillon*

Sun, Shade, or Both

Because of their site requirements, rain gardens tend to be sited in sunny locations. This is usually an advantage, since full to partial sun conditions offer more selections in the way of showy flowering plants like many of the native prairie plants that do so well in rain gardens. But don't shy away from constructing your rain garden in a shady spot if that is what you have. Shade gardens tend to be very showy in the springtime. In summer, they can turn into a beautiful display featuring varying textures, shapes, and shades of green.

Finally, if you choose to locate your garden in view of the street remember that rain gardens are a fairly new concept that many people have never heard of. Keeping your garden tidy and well maintained will go a long way toward convincing your neighbors that going green for rainwater is a great way to ensure a future of cleaner water.

Your rain garden should function for many years and will become a permanent part of your yard's landscape. Avoid future problems by installing your garden in a place where it will not become a liability down the road.

Calculating Your Water Load to Size Your Rain Garden

The average house size in the United States has nearly doubled over the past fifty years. Today's typical newly constructed home is now well over 2,300 square feet, and most home lots also contain a garage, driveway, and sidewalk. Add all the square footage together and you have a large proportion of a typical urban or suburban lot that is impervious to rainwater. Even a well-manicured lawn is an effective barrier to rainwater absorption compared to a natural meadow or a forest. All this points to the fact that most rainwater that falls on a typical home lot runs off the property instead of soaking into the ground.

Rainfall Runoff Table

The table below shows the runoff coefficient number or RCN of different land uses. The higher the RCN, the more runoff can be expected from the land use. Notice that both the soil type and the land use have a profound effect on the amount of runoff.

Land Use	Soil Type			
	Well Drained Sand or Gravel	Moderately Drained Coarse Soils	Poorly Drained Fine Textured Soils	Poorly Drained Clay Soil
Roofs, Paved Driveways	98	98	98	98
Agricultural Land	72	81	88	91
Grass Meadow (Mowed for Hay)	30	58	71	78
Forest with Brush Covering Ground	30	55	70	77
Open Space with Good Grass Cover (Lawn, Golf Course)	39	61	74	80
Residential Lot, 1/8 acre, 65% impervious	77	85	90	92
Residential Lot, 1/2 acre, 25% impervious	54	70	80	85

Rainwater that falls on the roof of a home or garage is usually collected by a system of gutters and directed to the ground via a downspout. Many downspouts empty onto the lawn where at least some of the water filters down into the soil. But often, the downspouts drain directly onto another impervious surface like a driveway where it is directed to the street or a grassed ditch and then into the neighborhood storm sewer system. The first step in sizing your rain garden is to decide how much rainwater runs off your property and how much of that water you wish to capture for your garden.

To calculate how many square feet of roof drains to each of your home's downspouts, simply multiply the length times the width of each section of roof that drains to each downspout. If you plan on directing the water from more than one downspout to your garden, you may add each separate section together to give you the total square feet that will supply the garden. Use the same calculation to determine the square footage of driveways, patios, or sidewalks where rainwater will run off into the garden.

An area of manicured turf grass lawn that is going to drain into your garden, especially if the soil underneath has been compacted by rolling or repeatedly driven on by a lawn tractor, needs to be accounted for in your sizing calculation. Compacted clay or silt soils that are covered with turf grass absorb very little rainwater, especially after a quick, heavy downpour. Add the square footage of any such grassed area that will drain into the spot you choose for your rain garden.

A thick lawn, especially one that sits atop compacted soil, can act as a barrier to rainwater.

Soil Type and Garden Size

If the soil of your rain garden is a well drained sandy loam or a recommended rain garden mix of sand, topsoil, and compost (see the section on soils on page 38), then your garden should be 20 to 30 percent the size of the drainage area. So, if your rain garden is taking run-off from a 20-foot by 30-foot section of roof (600 square feet) plus runoff from a 10-foot by 10-foot patio (100 square feet) for a total of 700 square feet, then your rain garden should be between 140 and 210 square feet in size. You can, of course, always make your garden larger, but to avoid drainage and flooding problems, the garden should never be smaller than 20 percent of the area that drains into it.

If the space that you select for your garden contains primarily poorly drained soil with lots of clay and silt and you choose not to augment the garden's soil with sand, topsoil, and/or compost, then the garden's area should be about 60 percent of the drainage area. This will compensate for the soil's slow percolation and will help you avoid issues with standing water in the garden.

A surprisingly large volume of water runs off a typical roof during a rainstorm. A rain garden captures this water that would otherwise run off your property and into the local storm sewer system.

How Many Gallons Is That?

Here is an easy way to calculate the number of gallons of water that run off of your roof or other impervious surface during a rainstorm. First, take the total number of square feet of impervious surface and multiply this number by the decimal inches of rain that fell during the rainstorm. Next, multiply that number by 0.623. This will give you the number of gallons of rainwater you saved to water your rain garden plants and recharge the groundwater.

As an example calculation, if you had runoff from a total of 2,000 square feet of roof and driveway that was going to your rain garden and a morning rainstorm produced a total of 1/2 inch of rain, then the number of gallons of water would be 2,000 x 0.50 x .623 = 623 gallons.

To get an appreciation of the volume of water that runs off your property in a year, multiply the total square feet of impervious surface on your property times the total annual inches of rainfall. Multiply this number by 0.623 to get the number of gallons of water per year.

Example: A 2,300 square foot home with a 15 by 30 foot paved drive and a 30 by 40 foot garage has a total of 3,950 square feet of impervious surface. In a typical year in southern Michigan, thirty-two inches of rain falls. The total annual runoff from our example homestead would be nearly 79,000 gallons of water.

Testing Your Site's Infiltration Rate (Percolation Test)

Once you have found the best spot in your yard for your rain garden and have established what type of soil you have, it is now time to see how well the existing soil absorbs water. There are several commercially available soil infiltration testing devices available, but these are really tools of the agricultural and scientific communities. For the purpose of a home rain garden, a simple test will tell you whether you need to change your garden's soil to help it better absorb water.

To see if you need to amend the soil in your rain garden to increase infiltration, dig a six-inch-deep hole with a shovel or post-hole digger in two or three spots within the rain garden's border and fill the holes with water. If the water in the hole soaks into the ground completely within twenty-four hours, the soil should work well without change. If the water does not infiltrate within a day, then it may be necessary to mix in sand, compost, or topsoil to increase the soil's ability to absorb water. The goal of a rain garden is to infiltrate water quickly into the ground and avoid having standing water on the ground's surface for a prolonged period (greater than twenty-four hours). Soil that has an infiltration rate greater than 1/4 inch of water per hour (or six inches in twenty-four hours) will work well as it is.

For the best results, do this test in the springtime or during the rainy season when the ground is fairly wet and not parched. If you do need to test an area during late summer or autumn when the ground is dry, give the area a good soaking before running the test.

A simple water percolation test is required to ensure the spot you choose for your garden is adequately drained.

A landscape professional uses a device called an infiltrometer to evaluate the soil's capacity to percolate water.

Obedient plant (*Physostegia virginiana*) will tolerate a wide range of soils.

Soil

Soils typically have four components: sand, silt, clay, and organic matter. The proportions of these ingredients largely determine the soil texture, which in turn determines other soil properties like fertility, porosity, and water retention. Sandy soils feel gritty and coarse, silty soils are smoother but not too sticky when wet, and clay soils are very sticky and clumpy when wet. Heavier clay soils hold more moisture and hold it longer; sandy soils drain faster.

Organic matter, also known as humus, is decomposing plant or animal material. It determines a soil's capacity to produce nitrogen, supports the community of soil microorganisms crucial to plant life, and retains bacterial byproducts like water and carbon dioxide. It also creates a moist, slightly acidic environment critical for the transfer of minerals from soil particles to plants.

Good soil is the most important factor in any type of gardening, but especially with rain gardens. It's definitely worth taking some time up front to get to know your soil. If you aren't sure of your soil type, have your soil tested by a soil-testing laboratory; check with your local university extension office for labs in your area. A soil test will provide you with information on existing soil texture, fertility, and pH level, along with recommendations on what to add to improve it.

Ideally the location you have chosen for your rain garden has a well-drained sandy soil with a pH of about 5.5 to 6.5. This will ensure proper drainage and allow you to grow a wide range of plants. However, if your soil is not suitable for a rain garden or the plants you want to use, there are some things you can do to improve the drainage, texture, and fertility, or to adjust the pH level. Your soil test results and your desired plant list will help determine just how much "soil engineering" you will need to do. Your goal is to create a loose, friable (easily crumbled) soil that drains well and that roots can penetrate so plants establish quickly.

Soil Texture

Even if your soil drains well (it passed your percolation test), it is still a good idea to add some organic matter to a new garden bed before planting. Organic matter always improves soil texture, adds valuable nutrients at a slow and steady pace, and has a buffering effect on soil pH. Also, a sandy soil will have a very low cationic exchange capacity, a measure of the soil's ability to hold plant nutrients. This ability for nutrients to readily wash through the sand can lead to contamination of ground water beneath the rain garden. Organic matter helps a sandy soil hold onto excess nutrients that plant roots don't take in.

The best source of organic matter for gardeners is compost. Composting materials like cow or horse manure, grass clippings, and leaves ensures that these materials will be in optimum condition to work into the soil. Other good sources of organic matter are well-rotted manure and chopped straw and hay. Avoid using peat-based products as soil amendments. The process of extracting peat from bogs is environmentally harmful to these threatened natural habitats. As with other soil changes, the easiest time to add organic matter is before planting a bed.

If your soil is heavy and drains poorly (high in clay), you will want to remove it and replace it with a soil that is permeable enough to allow water to drain and filter properly. Your replacement soil should be a mix of 50 to 60 percent coarse, sharp sand; 20 to 30 percent topsoil; and 20 to 30 percent organic matter. Ideally the topsoil will be a well-drained loam, but it can contain a small amount of clay (no more than 5 to 10 percent of the total mix). Clay particles absorb heavy metals, hydrocarbons, and other pollutants. Do not make the mistake of adding sand alone to clay soil; you will end up with a soil density similar to concrete.

A compost barrel in a garden. © Pack-Shot/ Shutterstock.com

A simple hand test will determine what type of soil you have at your rain garden site. The clay soil tested here formed a ribbon longer than one inch before breaking off.

Ribbon Test

You can also do a simple "ribbon test" to determine your soil type. Take a handful of soil and dampen it with water until it is moldable, like moist putty. Form the soil into a ball and place it between your thumb and forefinger, squeezing it into a ribbon of uniform thickness. Allow the ribbon to extend over your forefinger until it breaks from its own weight. If the soil cannot remain in a ball, you have sandy soil. If you can create a ribbon more than an inch long before it breaks, you have silty soil. If the soil forms a ribbon one to two inches long before it breaks, you have soil with lots of clay. If the soil makes a ribbon greater than two inches before it breaks, your soil is probably very heavy and poorly drained and not suitable for a rain garden.

Freshly composted earth from a compost bin.
© Stephen Rudolph/ Shutterstock.com

Soil Fertility

Plants require about fifteen different nutrients for growth and survival. The big three—nitrogen, phosphorous, and potassium—are required in substantial quantities and their presence is used to generally define soil fertility. If your soil test indicates you are significantly lacking in any of these elements, you may want to amend it before planting. Keep in mind, however, that native plants, especially prairie species, generally grow better in less-fertile soil than traditional garden plants do. Overly rich soils encourage the growth of weeds and can cause plants to grow too lushly and flop over. Most woodland shade plants require at least 40 percent organic matter in the soil.

To improve your overall soil fertility, add compost, well-rotted manure, fish emulsion, or "Milorganite." Improve soil nitrogen content by adding soybean meal, alfalfa meal, or compost. Soil phosphorus content can be increased by adding bone meal or rock phosphate, and potassium comes from granite dust, greensand, seaweed, or wood ashes. Be sure to follow your soil test recommendations carefully to avoid adding excess nutrients to your rain garden.

Soil pH

Soil acidity and alkalinity are measured in terms of pH on a scale from 1 to 14. A 7 on the scale indicates the soil is neutral in pH. Lower than 7, the soil is increasingly acidic; higher than 7, it is increasingly alkaline. Soil pH is important because it affects the availability of nutrients necessary for plant growth. It also affects microbial activity, which helps determine pollutant removal.

A soil pH of 5.5 to 6.5 is ideal for pollutant removal, which is convenient because that is the soil pH range preferred by most sun-loving prairie plants. Most soils fall into this range, but if your soil test indicates you are out of this range there are materials you can add. You can raise soil pH by adding agricultural lime, calcium, or wood ashes (in moderation). To get the desired slightly acidic soil most shade-loving woodland plants require, lower the soil pH by adding pine-needle or oak-leaf mulch, organic matter, ground oak leaves, gypsum or sulfur (in moderation).

Most woodland and shade plants prefer slightly acidic soils, so if your rain garden is in the shade, you may need to adjust soil pH before planting.

Washing a car on grass.

© *Shutterstock.com*

Good Housekeeping

There are many small things you can do every day that will add up to cleaner storm water and less water pollution. Most of these are simply a matter of practicing good housekeeping when it comes to storm water pollution prevention. Collectively, these are called administrative best management practices, or "BMPs" for short. Industrial and municipal workers use these administrative BMPs to keep pollution out of storm water. Many of these practices can also be use by homeowners who are interested in a cleaner environment.

Washing vehicles in the street or driveway is a common practice that has a negative impact on water quality. Vehicle wash water contains detergents, metals, oil, and sediment. If the wash water enters a storm drain, it will eventually carry its toxic load to the nearest river or stream, polluting the water and endangering the aquatic animals that live there.

Allowing wash water to enter a storm drain may also violate your community's Storm Water Permit (see sidebar page 12). The best practice is to wash your vehicle on a grassy area where the soaps and oils can be absorbed into the soil and eventually break down. Better yet, take your vehicle to the local car wash where dirty wash water is sent to the local treatment plant.

Keep grass clippings, leaves, and other yard waste out of storm drains. Keeping storm drains clear of such debris is a major headache for many cities and a huge problem for water quality. Rotting vegetation robs water of oxygen and can raise water temperature, a deadly combination for fish and the small animals they rely on for food. Never dump grass clippings or leaves near or into any water body. Instead, compost yard waste and apply the nutrient rich compost to your garden.

Keep fertilizers and pesticides out of storm water at all costs. The nutrients in fertilizer that make your lawn green will do the same thing to a pond or lake in the form of algae blooms and choking masses of underwater vegetation.

Most surface water has low nutrient levels that limit the growth of algae and water plants. When nutrient levels rise, so does the rate of plant growth. So much so that water plants take over, blocking out sunlight below the waters surface. When the plants die, they settle to the bottom and begin to decay. The resulting drop in oxygen levels creates dead zones in lakes and ponds.

Sweep up excess granules of fertilizer or pesticides that fall into the street or on the sidewalk. Never wash excess fertilizer, or any other spilled material, into the street or a storm drain. Apply lawn chemicals around water carefully, leaving a ten-foot buffer between the fertilized area and the water's edge.

It goes without saying that pet waste should be kept out of the storm drain, yet many owners fail to clean up after their pets, allowing waste to be washed into roadways and storm drains.

Pet waste is loaded with harmful bacteria that multiply quickly when suspended in water, especially in the summer. Pet waste contamination is a prime suspect in many beach closings where bacteria levels rise to levels that threaten human health. Help keep our water clean by cleaning up after your pet and disposing of the waste properly.

Many dangerous substances wind up in storm drains simply because people don't realize that storm water is not treated before it discharges into a river or lake. Materials like paint, motor oil, solvents, and other chemicals spread quickly through the storm drain system and even small amounts can contaminate large areas downstream. Remember the best policy to prevent pollution is "only rain in the drain."

Pet waste sign at the park.
© Kevin Giszewski/Shutterstock.com

BUILDING YOUR RAIN GARDEN

You have chosen to make the world a little greener,

and now it's time to turn your vision into reality.

A well-planned rain garden project will go smoothly if

you keep a few things in mind. As with any task, many

hands make light work. Take the opportunity to turn

a chore into a party by enlisting the help of family,

friends, and neighbors. Often, the promise of a free

meal is enough to draw a crowd of helpers.

Let everyone know the environmental benefits your

rain garden will bring and who knows, maybe you can

give in return when they decide to build their

very own rain gardens.

A rain garden takes just a short time to install, but the benefits can last for years. Rain gardens are a good investment in water quality as well as a haven for colorful wildlife.

A few simple yard tools are all that you need to construct a rain garden. *Illustration by Simeon Cochrane*

If you plan to dig the garden by hand, please remember to work within your limitations. Although it is possible to do so, you do not need to finish your rain garden in just one afternoon or even one weekend. Stretch the project out if need be and keep it fun; there is no need to work yourself into sore muscles or achy joints just to "get 'er done."

Finally, work safely. Drink plenty of fluids, take a break when you need it, and use caution when working with tools. Use your legs, not your back, when lifting heavy loads; wear sturdy shoes and protective gloves. Remember, a job done safely is a job well done.

Tools

Here is a list of tools that you will need for your rain garden project. Remember, quality tools are always a good investment, so don't waste money on tools that won't stand up to the job.

Spade-style shovel
Square-point shovel
Heavy-duty wheelbarrow
Landscape rake
Mallet or small sledgehammer
25- to 50-foot garden hose
Chalk line
Mason twine
Open-reel measuring tape
Survey stakes (16- or 24-inch)
Spirit level (4- to 6-foot)
String level
Heavy plastic tarp
2x4 board, 6 to 8 feet long

Some power tools that may make the job easier include:
Garden tiller
Small backhoe
Skid steer
Trencher
Sod cutter

Other supplies that may come in handy down the road include:
Straw mat erosion blanket (to establish grass on a berm)
Hand trowel (for planting)
Post-hole digger (for fence posts if the garden will be fenced)
Large scoop shovel (for loading compost and mulch)

Rain Barrels

Watering a flower or vegetable garden is expensive. Water has become a major household expense and in some cases, has been subject to rationing during dry spells. The perfect solution to high water bills is to store rainwater for a sunny day.

Rain barrels are nothing new; people have been collecting rain and using the water for drinking, cooking, and irrigation for centuries. With today's emphasis on conserving water and saving money, collecting and saving rain has made a huge comeback. Installing a rain barrel makes perfect environmental and economic sense.

Most rain barrels are made of high quality, molded plastic and will hold fifty to eighty gallons of water. A good quality rain barrel will have several features. The stopcock fitting on the bottom of the barrel should fit a typical garden hose and the unit should have a built in overflow that discharges excess water. A fine mesh screen on the top of the rain barrel will prevent mosquitoes from turning your stored water into a nursery.

The higher your rain barrel is installed, the better. Higher elevation equals greater water pressure coming out of the barrel. That means that water from the barrel will travel further and faster through your garden hose. You won't get enough pressure to use a sprayer nozzle, but with enough head on the water you may be able to use a soaker hose to water a garden across the yard.

You can leave a rain barrel in place year-round in colder climates as long as you leave the stopcock open and keep the barrel drained. Frozen water expands and may burst the rain barrel if it is not emptied before temperatures drop below freezing. If you installed a flexible hose connection from your downspout to fill the barrel, move the hose aside during colder months to keep the water out. Covering the top of the barrel will also help keep it dry during the winter.

BELOW LEFT: Installing a rain barrel above ground level on a deck or large porch increases the water pressure or "head."

BELOW RIGHT: Failure to winterize your rain barrel may lead to cracking or other severe damage.
© Dan Christian

Topsoil, compost, sand, and mulch can be purchased by the cubic yard (or simply yard) from local landscape material suppliers who will deliver right to the jobsite.

Raw Materials

In Chapter 1, we discussed soil testing and how to decide if you need to enhance the soil of your rain garden to increase its ability to absorb water. If you already have well drained soil, the garden will require only a dressing of compost and a covering of mulch. On slow draining sites, soil enhancement with a mixture of compost, topsoil, and sharp sand will be necessary to increase the garden's ability to absorb and hold water.

The amount of compost, topsoil, and sharp sand you need will depend on the size of the rain garden and the depth of the replacement soil mixture. The table on the next page shows how much of each material you will need based on the garden's size and the amount of soil removed and replaced with a 60/20/20 mixture of sharp sand, compost, and topsoil.

If you have your materials delivered in advance, store them under a tarp to prevent rain from washing soils or mulch into the street. Do not pile materials or spoil piles near a storm drain inlet. If this is unavoidable, place a temporary cover on the inlet to prevent the material from entering the storm drain. Always sweep up any leftover or spilled material and never wash soil or mulch into the storm drain.

Materials Table*

Garden size (sq. ft)	2–3 inch topping of mulch or compost	Depth of replacement soil	Sharp Sand (60%)	Compost (20%)	Topsoil (20%)
100 sq. feet	1 yard**	12 inches (1 ft)	2 yards	20 bags	20 bags
e.g., 10 ft x 10 ft		18 inches (1.5 ft)	3.5 yards	1 yard	1 yard
5 ft x 20 ft		24 inches (2 ft)	4.5 yards	1.5 yards	1.5 yards
150 sq. ft	1.5 yards	12 inches (1 ft)	3.5 yards	1 yard	1 yard
e.g., 10 ft x 15 ft		18 inches (1.5 ft)	5 yards	1.5 yards	1.5 yards
		24 inches (2 ft)	6.5 yards	2 yards	2 yards
200 sq. ft.	2 yards	12 inches (1 ft)	4.5 yards	1.5 yards	1.5 yards
e.g., 10 ft x 20 ft		18 inches (1.5 ft)	6.5 yards	2 yards	2 yards
		24 inches (2 ft)	9 yards	3 yards	3 yards
300 sq. ft	3 yards	12 inches (1 ft)	6.5 yards	2 yards	2 yards
e.g., 10 ft x 30 ft		18 inches (1.5 ft)	10 yards	3.5 yards	3.5 yards
15 ft x 20 ft		24 inches (2 ft)	13 yards	4.5 yards	4.5 yards

* For practical purposes, the values in the table are rounded off to the nearest ½ yard.

** One yard is equal to 27 cubic feet and is equivalent to 27 one-cubic-foot bags of material.

Constructing a rain garden becomes an expensive and time-consuming task on a site that does not percolate water or is often under water for several days following a rainstorm. Such a site will require complete soil replacement plus the installation of an under drain if it is to function properly. A large project like this is best left to a professional landscaper with the proper tools.

Storage Area

Most rain gardens are designed to capture the runoff from up to an inch of rainfall. The majority of storms produce less than one inch of rain, so a garden designed to the one-inch standard should work well just about anywhere. There is no need to over-design your garden to hold the runoff from larger storms. During rare storms that threaten to overload the garden, the excess water will exit via the overflow.

Remember that rain gardens are built in a shallow depression. The distance from the top of the garden's berm to the top of the mulch is the garden's storage area. This area holds water for a short time until it can soak into the garden's soil. The depth of the storage area is based on collecting the standard one inch of rainfall and, as stated before, is determined by the area of surface drained into the garden and the garden's size.

To calculate how deep your garden's storage area should be, you need to account for run-off from both your roof or driveway (impervious) and any grassy areas (pervious) that flow into the garden. You can estimate that 95 percent of the water that falls on a roof or driveway will run off while 15 percent of the water that falls on your lawn will run off. Based on this, you can calculate the storage depth as:

Storage Depth= (0.95 x impervious area) + (0.15 x pervious area) ÷ Garden Area

For example, if you were planning to install a 200-square-foot garden that captures water from a 600-square-foot section of roof plus 600 square feet of lawn, then the storage area would be:

Storage Depth= (0.95 x 600) + (0.15 x 600) ÷ 200 = 3.3 inches (round up to 4 inches).

Storage depths between four and twelve inches work well for most rain gardens. You can also adjust the garden's size accordingly to achieve a storage depth within the four- to twelve-inch range.

Hummingbirds and many other types of wildlife benefit from rain gardens.
© Diane Denning

Berm · Storage · Replacement Soil · Storage · Native Soil

A rain garden in cross section showing the garden's storage area, berm, replacement soil, and deep-rooted native plants.

Illustration by Simeon Cochrane

Sketching It Up

Now that you have found the perfect spot in your yard for your rain garden, it is time to draw it up on paper and lay out the garden's boundaries on the ground. Drawing the garden out on paper gives you real dimensions to work from. A drawing will also allow you to visualize and choose a shape for the garden that fits well into your landscaping. It is not necessary to make a scaled drawing, but one done on graph paper with larger-sized squares will allow you to show the garden's relative dimensions more easily.

Your drawing should include not only the dimensions of the garden itself, but also distances from the edges and center of the garden to reference points like the house, driveway, or other permanent structures. Mark underground utilities, lawn-sprinkler heads, and other items to avoid during construction as well. Sketch in any inflow pipes or channels as well as overflow structures. Flow arrows showing the direction of any overland flow into the garden will help you to place the berm in the right location.

A cut-away side view sketch of the garden may be useful if you are building on a slope. Remember that to work efficiently, a rain garden must be level at the bottom of the excavation. This means that when your garden is built on an incline you will be removing more soil on the up-slope side of the garden than on the down-slope side. A cutaway view will show exactly how much soil to remove along each section of the garden.

Laying It Out

Once you have everything down on paper, you are ready to locate the garden in your yard and mark out its boundary. The easiest way to lay out the boundaries of an irregularly shaped garden is with a length of garden hose. Working from your sketch, locate the edge of the garden on the ground and simply lay out the garden's dimensions with the length of hose. When the shape looks right, either snap a chalk line around the perimeter or just leave the hose in place and start digging.

If using a garden hose to lay out the garden's boundaries is impractical or if you want a more precise layout, you can also stake the garden out. For this task, you will need a mallet or small sledgehammer, some mason's twine, a chalk line, an open-reel measuring tape, and about a dozen wooden survey stakes. For a round garden, start by locating the approximate center of the garden and driving a stake into this point. You can measure from two reference points in your yard to find the exact center, but most of the time eyeballing the center will do just fine.

Set the perimeter of the garden by measuring four equally distant points from the center at the 3, 6, 9, and 12 o'clock positions. Each point should be one-half the total diameter of the garden. Place a stake at each position.

When you have staked the four points around the center, connect the stakes with mason's twine, leaving a little slack in the line.

Working around the original four points, measure the middle distance between each neighboring stake. Pull the mason's twine out at the middle point to round out the garden's shape. Hold the line in place with a stake at each of these four intermediate points.

When all eight stakes are in place, you will have the outline of your rain garden. Using the circular configuration as a starting point, you can also create an oval-shaped garden, a crescent-shaped garden, a kidney-shaped garden, or any shape in between by simply moving the stakes and twine.

Removing Existing Vegetation

The first step in installing your garden will be to remove any existing vegetation from the spot you have chosen. Removing the vegetation from a perennial flowerbed that will be turned into a rain garden will simply require that the existing plants be dug up and moved to a new location. If you no longer need of any of the healthy perennials that you must move, be sure to check with neighbors and friends to see if they have a spot for the plants before you discard them.

Removing sod or well-established grass from a site can be a bit more labor intensive, but with the right tools, it should go quickly. The best hand tool for removing sod is a square-point shovel. Sod grass roots are usually less than four inches deep, so you should be able to remove large sections by inserting the shovel a short way into the ground and pushing it along just under the roots. Sectioning off long segments of sod with the edge of your shovel will allow you to peel off large strips. Simply roll up the strips of sod as you go along. Do not discard strips of quality sod if you have a bare spot in your lawn or another place where they might be useful.

There are several machines designed to remove sod or grass. Check your local rental store to see what they have available for short-term rental.

Applying herbicide to kill the grass before you begin will make things go faster. Use a glycol-phosphate herbicide like Round-Up or a similar product to kill the existing grass. These herbicides break down a short time after application and won't linger in the soil. Be sure to follow the manufacturer's instructions when using any herbicide.

A more environmentally friendly way to kill grass is to cover the area with black plastic for about a week before digging. This will also keep the soil beneath moist and make digging much easier.

To remove established sod by hand, push a square-point shovel just beneath the roots and lift the sod up as you go along.

With the vegetation removed, it is easier to see the final shape of the garden. Now is the time to make final adjustments to the garden's size and shape.

Most lawns will have a layer of topsoil just below the sod. Carefully dig out the topsoil layer and set it aside. You can use this soil for the garden's berm or mix it back into the garden with your other soil amendments.

Digging It Out

Once you have laid out your garden and removed the existing vegetation, it is time to start digging. How much digging you do will depend on the size of your garden, the slope of your yard, and the amount of soil that you replace.

Things will go smoothly if you remember a few basic rules. Moving piles of dirt around is a lot of work, so have a plan in place before you start digging. Set aside topsoil and loam to use for the garden's berm and remove unwanted soil to a predetermined, out-of-the-way spot. Dig from the outside of the garden toward the inside, work within your limitations, and keep the work area free of hazards. Most importantly, do not start digging unless your local one-call utility hotline (8-1-1) has flagged all your underground utilities.

Rain gardens built on soil that infiltrates water quickly will require only a dressing of topsoil or compost and a covering of mulch to function properly.

If you have well-drained native soil and your garden needs only a dressing of topsoil and a covering of mulch, you will only need to dig out enough to form the storage area of the garden. Be sure to account for any topping of compost, topsoil, or mulch that you will add and adjust the depth of the storage area accordingly.

If you are replacing the native soil with the 60/20/20 rain garden mixture of sharp sand, compost, and topsoil, you will need to dig out enough for the storage area plus the depth of the replacement soil.

The soil replacement depth depends on several things. If your native soil is well drained, but contains a large proportion of clay, replace six to twelve inches of soil with the rain garden soil mixture. Think of this as insurance against the soil becoming compacted from all the excess water that your garden will take in. The rain garden mixture will also provide better growing conditions than the native soil, so your plants will do better.

Compost contains microorganisms and fungi that are essential to healthy plant growth.

Remove native soil consisting of heavy clay or other poorly draining materials to a depth of eighteen to twenty-four inches. These soils have little internal pore space, so they do not store water well. Poorly drained soil will cause water to pond on the surface of the garden instead of soaking in. The rain garden mixture acts like a sponge that holds water until it can infiltrate into the subsoil.

The depth of the soil replacement can also influence the amount of water a rain garden can hold. Up to 40 percent of the volume of the rain garden soil mixture is available to hold water, so you can increase the garden's capacity by increasing the depth of the amended soil mixture.

Working from the edge toward the middle, begin digging out the garden. If the garden is on a slope, begin digging at the upslope side.

When you have finished your excavation, use a spirit level on a 6-to-8-foot-long 2x4-inch board to make sure the bottom is level from front to back and side to side. Leveling helps the garden infiltrate water evenly. When the garden is level, loosen the remaining subsoil. Tilling to a depth of five to six inches is the best way to "fluff" the under-soil. If you do not have access to a garden tiller, loosen the soil with a spade or rake. This small step will go a long way toward helping the subsoil absorb water and encourage vigorous, deep root growth.

Before adding replacement soil, you may want to check the infiltration rate at the bottom of the excavation. Using the same infiltration test described in Chapter 1, test several spots around the bottom. If the water does not infiltrate the subsoil within seventy-two hours, you may need to reduce the amount of water directed to the garden or install an under drain system to remove excess water.

Beginning at the edge of the garden, remove the under soil.

The depth of the garden should include both the storage area and the depth of the soil amendments. When the excavation is complete, make sure the bottom of the garden is level. Roughing up the bottom of the excavation with a garden tiller or rake will help your plants establish deep, healthy roots.

Soil amendments can be added individually and mixed together as you go along, or they may be pre-mixed outside the garden and added to the excavation.

Mixing It Up

There are several ways to prepare your replacement soil mix. It may be easiest to add three wheelbarrow loads of sand and one load each of compost and topsoil at a time to the excavation and mix them as you go along. As you mix the soils together, spread them evenly across the bottom of the excavation. Do not compact or tamp down the new soil, as this will lessen its ability to infiltrate water.

You may also pre-mix your soil before adding it to the excavation. This method may be easier for a smaller garden where space to work in the excavation is limited. As above, minimize soil compaction by limiting the number of people walking on the newly added soil mixture.

If you are adding inflow or overflow piping inside the garden, now is the time to do so. Outside piping from downspouts or to overflows can be hooked up later if need be.

To give your new plants a nutrient boost, top the replacement mixture with several inches of compost. Smooth the top of the garden into a shallow concave bowl. Creating a slight depression around the center of the garden will keep the soil there slightly wetter than the rest of the garden and create a perfect home for water-loving plants.

French Drains

Drainage woes around building foundations plague many homeowners, and the consequences can be dire. Leaking basements, standing water after a rainstorm, and sewage backups due to older or leaking tiles are just a few of the headaches. Fixing a drainage problem around your home or on your property can be expensive, or it may be as simple as installing a French drain.

A French drain is a time-proven, zero energy way to move excess water away from buildings or drain a low area in your yard. *Illustration by Simeon Cochrane*

It's Not Really French

French drains have been solving drainage problems since the mid-nineteenth century when Henry French, a Harvard-trained lawyer and Yankee farmer, published an insightful book on farm drainage. Among his many ideas for keeping your land (and your cellar) high and dry was the use of a simple, rock-filled trench that, through no power other than gravity, moved ground water to a more desirable location. While the use of modern materials like perforated pipe and permeable landscape cloth have tweaked the performance of French drains, the process remains essentially unchanged.

If the existing slope in your yard is relatively steep, the trench for the drain may only need to be a couple of feet deep. Other circumstances may require a deeper trench with enough slope to move the water along. Usually a slope of 1 percent is steep enough (one foot drop per 100 feet of run, see section on calculating slope in Chapter 1).

Materials

To construct a French drain you will need the following materials:

- garden spade
- pickaxe
- wheelbarrow
- permeable landscape fabric
- perforated rigid 4-inch plastic drain pipe (Do not use flexible pipe; it is impossible to clean if it becomes clogged, and it is easier to set the proper slope with rigid pipe.)
- clean, washed gravel—enough to fill the trench
- string level
- mason's twine
- 2 survey stakes
- tape measure
- trencher or backhoe (for longer and deeper drains or heavier soils)

Planning It Out

First, decide where you want the water to go, keeping in mind that wherever it goes, it should not cause problems for your neighbors or create an unwanted wet area elsewhere in your yard. French drains can empty to a variety of places, including into your rain garden, into underground cisterns, into drainage swales, or, if your grading allows, out to the ground surface where the water can spread out over your lawn. When you have decided on a path for the drain, contact your local one-call utility location hotline (see the sidebar on page 25) to locate any hidden underground utilities before digging.

Dig It

Excavate the trench for a short-run French drain using a garden spade and a pick to break up compacted or heavy soil. A longer drain may require a trenching machine or a back-hoe. A wider excavation will allow you to get your feet, hands, and tools inside the trench and will drain better than a narrow trench.

Using the mason's twine, string level, and your two survey stakes, set up a level line along the edge of the excavation. As you dig the trench, measure down from level to make sure the trench is properly sloped. Remember that the soil you remove will be replaced with gravel, so remove the excavated soil as you go along.

Once the trench is complete, there are several options for laying out the drainpipe, landscape fabric, and gravel. One option is to line the trench itself with pervious landscape fabric, put a layer of gravel in the bottom of the lined trench, place the drainpipe on the gravel with the perforations facing downward, and fill in the trench with the rest of the gravel. This option works best for relatively short and shallow French drains.

A second option is to wrap the drainpipe in pervious landscape fabric and lay it down on top of a layer of washed gravel in the bottom of the trench. Fill in the trench with the remainder of the gravel as above. Make sure the pipe is oriented with the perforations facing down.

You may also choose to omit the drainpipe entirely and rely only on the gravel to convey the water. As long as your trench is properly sloped, this option should work fine. Lining the trench with porous landscape fabric before applying the gravel will keep out fine soil particles and improve the lifespan of the drain. Completely enclose the gravel in porous landscape fabric to create a tube of gravel that extends the length of the drain.

To keep dirt, debris, and small animals out of the drainpipe, cap the downstream end with a perforated cap or cover the end with a piece of porous landscape fabric secured with a hose clamp.

Finishing Touches

Cover the surface of the French drain trench with decorative gravel and edge with pavers to make a walkway. To hide the French drain, cover the trench with several inches of top-soil and lay down sod. To keep the water flowing nicely and the drainpipe free of clogs, do not use deeply rooted plants over the drain.

Overflows

Your rain garden is designed to handle the water from one inch of rain. In many parts of the country, a storm of this size or larger happens several times a year. Chances are that sometime, more rain will fall than your garden can handle. Make sure you prepare for this by installing an overflow in your garden. An overflow allows you to control where the excess water will go and prevents your garden from washing out during a heavy downpour.

Every rain garden should have some type of overflow. These can be as simple as a notch or a pipe installed in the berm that allows water above a certain level to escape. Installing a standing pipe inside the garden to collect water above a certain level and direct it out onto the grass or street works well. Keep critters and debris out of overflow pipes by covering both ends with a perforated cap or screen.

A rock-lined channel through a small section of the berm makes an excellent overflow. By using large, decorative stones atop a bed of smaller stones to line the channel, the overflow not only looks nice but also prevents erosion by slowing water as it travels out of the garden and down the channel.

If you have a catch basin on your property that connects to the storm drain, this may be a great place to install a rain garden with a built-in overflow. Catch basins are located in a low spot so that they collect the runoff water from streets and sidewalks. Surrounding the catch basin with a rain garden allows some water to soak back into the soil instead of flowing down the drain. Make sure the garden sits below the rim on the catch basin to keep soil and mulch out of the structure.

No matter what style you choose, plan to install the overflow while you are constructing the garden. Having all the materials beforehand (piping, fittings, glue, etc.) will keep things moving along.

If you have a catch basin in your yard that is attached to a public storm drain, you can either build a rain garden around the structure or direct your overflow to it.

OPPOSITE: An overflow directs excess water from an extreme rain event safely out of the garden.

Gray Water

Conserving water is a modern-day necessity. As the population grows and spreads, so does the demand for clean water.

America's love affair with ornamental garden and household plants keeps our homes and neighborhoods beautiful, but the care of these plants consumes huge amounts of drinking-quality water each year. By using gray water instead of drinking water to irrigate your plants, you can have your flowers and save money too.

Gray water is simply "slightly used" water that is not suitable for drinking or cooking but is safe enough to use for irrigation. Gray water includes water from dishwashing or from the washing machine. It can also include condensate from air conditioners or dehumidifiers and water from fish tanks or pet bowls. In fact, any water that does not contain human waste (known as "black water") qualifies as gray water. Black water contains dangerous bacteria and is never suitable for watering plants.

It is best to use gray water only on ornamental plants. If you do decide to water vegetables with gray water, apply the water directly to the ground surrounding the plant and avoid splashing water on the leaves. Do not use gray water to irrigate root crops like carrots or potatoes, or on leafy vegetables like spinach.

Collecting gray water can be as simple as placing the condensate hose from an air conditioner in a bucket or as complex as re-routing your existing plumbing to collect bathwater from your tub. If you are collecting water from a dehumidifier or an inside air conditioner, avoid messy overflows by checking your reservoir regularly.

An inventory of water use in your home will reveal many sources of gray water.

The plumbing in many green-design homes collects gray and black water separately and incorporates gray water into landscape irrigation. Often, gray water is collected in a separate sump or cistern that can be pumped out as needed.

Gray water may contain soaps and other cleaning products, but most of these will break down into plant food after a short time in the soil. However, you should avoid products that contain chlorine bleach or boron.

Use water that contains products that include sodium salts (as many laundry softeners do) sparingly. Salts can build up in the soil and create alkaline conditions that are toxic to many plants, especially those that need acidic soil like rhododendrons and azaleas. It is always a good idea to give the garden a dose of fresh water occasionally to keep salt from building up in the soil.

Dishwashers are a great source for gray water.
© Alexander Raths/ Shutterstock.com

Porous Pavement

Rainwater that runs off sidewalks and driveways causes many environmental problems, but what if water passed right through these surfaces instead? Several types of paving blocks are available that do just that. Even more amazing, there is a method for pouring concrete that does the same thing.

Two types of paving block allow the passage of rainwater into the soil below. Permeable pavers look like normal pavers but are installed to allow water pass through spaces between the blocks. These are best suited for patios and other areas that receive only foot traffic. Porous pavers are pavers with built-in holes through which water will drain. After installing porous pavers, fill the holes with soil and seed with grass. The holes can also be filled with aggregate. This type of paver can handle heavy loads and is suitable for driveways and parking areas.

Porous concrete uses a carefully controlled mixture of cement and water that glues small stones (aggregate) together while leaving many spaces or pores for water to pass through. One square foot of properly installed porous pavement can infiltrate over five gallons of water per minute.

Porous concrete works well in colder climates. The spaces in the concrete trap air, allowing the pavement to hold heat better than regular concrete. This means that snow tends to melt rather than collect when it lands on porous concrete. To work well in a cold climate, porous concrete must be installed over well-drained substrate or a system of underground drainage pipes. If water trapped under the concrete freezes, the concrete will no longer infiltrate water and may be damaged by frost heave.

Water poured on a porous concrete sidewalk on Toledo, Ohio's Maywood Street passes through the concrete instead of running off.

Most homes have at least a couple of downspouts that collect rainwater from the gutter system. Downspouts that release water to the street or driveway are a great source of irrigation for a rain garden.

Connecting the Downspout

Many small rain gardens only collect runoff water from a section of driveway, sidewalk, or patio. The main source of water for most rain gardens, however, is runoff from a roof. If you have ever watched rainwater pour out of a downspout during a heavy rain, you know that gutters are very efficient water collectors. As we saw in Chapter 1, a roof sheds a tremendous amount of water during a heavy rain, and this is the bounty you want to capture for your rain garden.

There are many ways to connect a downspout to your rain garden. Connect a downspout that is relatively close to the garden with a short length of flexible plastic pipe. Your local home center or hardware store sells both the piping and the fitting that connects to the end of the downspout. Bury the pipe in a shallow trench to hold it in place and keep it out from under foot.

An easy way to connect your downspout to your rain garden is with a length of corrugated plastic pipe. For convenience and safety, bury the pipe underground, taking care to slope it toward the rain garden.

A trenching machine or "Ditch Witch" is a handy way to bury a longer length of pipe. Most equipment rental stores will rent them for a day at a reasonable price. Have the location of your trench laid out beforehand to save time and make certain your one-call utility hotline has cleared the area you trench.

In some yards, a shallow, grassy or rock-strewn swale is the perfect solution to getting the water from the downspout to the garden. Use your imagination and work the swale into your existing landscape to create an interesting feature instead of a simple water-conveyance channel. Border the swale with ferns or other decorative plants to create a hidden rainwater stream.

Remember that water collected from a roof will be moving fast when it hits the rain garden, so you will need to slow it down with an energy dissipater. The easiest way to slow the flow and allow the water to spread slowly and evenly into the garden is to place a small pile of rocks at the pipe outlet. Pop-up irrigators are another great way to distribute the water slowly and evenly and these worked very well in our demonstration garden (see photo).

To bury longer lengths of pipe, a trench excavator or "Ditch Witch" does the job quickly and neatly.

Pop-up valves attached to the inflow pipe disperse water slowly and evenly into the garden.

Installing the Berm

A rain garden berm is simply a low wall of soil surrounding the down-slope half of the garden. The berm works like a dam, holding water in the garden until it can be absorbed. A rain garden installed on gently sloping terrain will need a shorter berm than a garden built on a steep incline.

Make the berm as tall as the rise from the back of the garden to the front. That is, if you measure a rise of one foot over the length of the garden, the berm should be one foot tall. Do not extend the raised berm all the way around the garden, which would prevent overland flow from entering the garden.

The berm should be tallest along the rear of the garden with a gentle taper up each side to enclose the down-slope side of the garden in a semi-circle. Measure the height of the berm from the final elevation of the soil not including the layer of mulch. Using a string level or a sufficiently long 2x4 board and a spirit level, check to make sure the top of the berm is level with the ground at the up-slope side of the garden.

To form the berm, first remove any vegetation from the area. Build the berm up in layers, tamping the soil down as you go along. The back of a shovel or the flat side of a rake works well for this. Continue adding layers of soil until the berm is formed. Sculpt the berm into a gently sloping, tapered semi-circle with a landscape rake.

There are several options for covering the berm. Whatever cover you choose, make sure to protect any bare soil until you get your cover in place. This will prevent wind or rain from eroding the berm.

Cover the berm with mulch for easy maintenance. Choose mulch that will stick together, such as pine straw or shredded bark. This type of mulch will not migrate downhill during a downpour and expose the bare soil at the top of the berm.

A berm around the down-slope side of your garden will help hold water until it can be absorbed into the soil. If your garden is built on a sloping surface, a berm is essential for the garden to properly function.

You can also seed the berm with grass. Typical sod grass works well as do some of the shorter native perennial varieties like little bluestem. If you seed the berm instead of transplanting live plants, cover the berm with an erosion blanket until the seeds take root. A covering of mulch will help control erosion until transplanted live plants take hold.

Many types of low-growing ground cover plants are suitable for planting on the berm. Wild strawberry will spread quickly and cover the berm with low, bright green leaves and delicious, tiny red fruit. Several varieties of groundcover sedums are available that grow low, spread quickly, and produce tiny bright flowers in season.

Pine straw mulch holds together well in the rain and wind and makes an excellent low-maintenance cover for a berm.

Planting low-growing, perennial groundcover plants like wild strawberry (*Fragaria*) on the berm can provide a quick-spreading and beautiful covering.

Money and other
forms of assistance
are available to
homeowners who wish
to install a rain garden
on their properties.

Incentives and Grant Money

If you are considering installing a rain garden but are hedging at the cost, help may be just a grant application away. Environmental Protection Agency regulations have put many communities under the gun to do a better job managing storm-water runoff, and public participation is crucial to success. One proven way to get the public involved is to offer incentives to individual homeowners to improve the quality of stormwater leaving their property.

Large and small communities around the country offer homeowners incentive programs to install rain gardens on their property. These programs are a win-win proposition for local government and for their constituents. For government, the program satisfies EPA requirements for cleaner water. For his or her part, the homeowner receives a financial bonus in the form of a cash payment or a tax incentive.

How do you get in on this? Contact your local city or county government and ask if they have a rain garden incentive program. Conservation districts, local watershed councils, or nongovernment conservation groups also administer programs. Payment can range up to several hundred dollars and can be available as cash payments, matching grant funds, or tax incentives.

Municipal and Commercial Rain Gardens

Rain gardens line Michigan Avenue, the principal route to Michigan's historic capital building.

Many cities, towns, and businesses install rain gardens to reduce their storm water footprint. Commercial and municipal rain gardens are used to treat storm water from large impervious areas like parking lots, commercial building roofs, and streets. Incorporating a rain garden into the landscaping of a shopping or residential district enhances curb appeal and sends a message that clean water is important in the community.

In the high price urban real estate market, start-up businesses pay hundreds of dollars per square foot for development land in prime locations. In a location where the municipal storm water system is undersized due to unexpected growth or the amount of storm water runoff is tightly regulated, adding structures like storm water ponds or wetlands to deal with excess runoff can consume valuable real estate.

A common solution is to incorporate one or more rain gardens into the property's landscaping. Rain gardens will reduce the amount of storm water running off the property without taking up extra space. Municipal rain gardens can often be melded into existing storm water structures, especially if they are installed during street construction projects.

A commercial or municipal rain garden will always have an under drain system to prevent the garden from flooding. The under drain consists of a perforated pipe covered with a layer of gravel or pea-stone laid at the bottom of the garden beneath the replacement soil. The under drain pipe is connected to the city storm drain system. Excess water passes into the pipe and is removed via the normal storm drain system.

The soil in developed, urban areas is generally highly compacted from human activity and does not absorb rainfall very well. Natural soil in urban areas is often removed and replaced by a thin layer of topsoil on which turf grass is grown. Poor drainage, compacted soil, and low soil quality spell failure for rain gardens.

Replacement soil should always be used in commercial and municipal rain gardens. This not only ensures a well-drained garden but also supplies the rain garden plants with the nutrients they need to thrive in an urban setting.

Because it is especially important to use plants that are adapted to local conditions and extremes, plants used in rain gardens that drain streets and parking areas must be chosen carefully.

In northern regions where roads and sidewalks are salted in the winter, rain garden plants must tolerate salty soils. This is especially true of plants in the garden near the point where rainwater enters from the street. Cold weather stresses plants too, so check planting zone requirements carefully.

Summer heat in many urban areas, especially in the southern United States, can wilt plants that are not adapted to high temperatures. Pollution from automobiles and from human activity also stresses plants, so the hardiest and toughest varieties usually do the best.

Rain gardens are a relatively new feature, and winning over public opinion is important. Public gardens should not look weedy or overgrown and must be kept free of trash and litter. A small sign or plaque showing how a rain garden works and the benefits of clean storm water will help the public appreciate and understand the garden.

Newly constructed rain gardens collect street runoff on Toledo, Ohio's Maywood Avenue.

A rain garden in full bloom adds visual interest to an office building in Lansing, Michigan.

A large rain garden adorns a public park in East Lansing, Michigan's Towar neighborhood.

Creating a Swale Garden

In many neighborhoods, a swale or ditch collects rainwater from roads and sidewalks. A well-maintained swale can improve water quality by slowing down runoff and allowing rainwater to seep into the ground. Unfortunately, a poorly maintained swale works against clean water.

Even though a swale may be in the public right-of-way, the home-owner is often responsible for its upkeep. Before installing a garden in a swale, check with the city or township to be sure it doesn't violate any ordinance. Also, check to see who is responsible for mowing. If the city or township does the mowing, you may need to post the swale as a "no-mow zone" to alert mowing crews.

Many swales are mowed to the same height as a lawn, or the vegetation is removed altogether leaving nothing but bare soil. While this treatment may help remove storm water quickly, it is also a rec-ipe for trouble. Why not put your ditch or swale to work to improve water quality instead of degrading it? With a little work and some native plants, you can turn a roadside swale into a beautiful roadside garden that purifies rainwater runoff.

Closely mown vegetation in a swale reduces its ability to hold soil in place. This can lead to erosion that widens and deepens the channel. Close-cropped vegetation also does nothing to slow down storm water as it races to the nearest stream, carrying with it all the toxins it has washed off the road. Killing all the vegetation in a swale leaves nothing to hold the soil in place and only hastens the erosion process.

If water from a downpour moves rapidly through the swale, you need to slow it down and give it a chance to soak into the ground. The best way to do this is to put a series of water energy dissipaters in place on the upstream end. This can be as simple as placing a few stones in the upstream flow channel. Do not try to block the flow as this may cause water to back up and flood the roadway or your neighbor's yard. You only want to slow things down a bit.

Many people dislike swales because they tend to store water and encourage mosquitoes. If your swale holds water, you may wish to level out any low spots and re-grade it into a gentle slope. Just like a rain garden, you can enhance the soil in your swale to help it absorb water. Absorption and uptake of rainwater will improve as native plants mature.

Removing all vegetation from a swale causes severe erosion and degrades water quality.

Adding vegetation to a swale that drains into a catch basin cleanses runoff before it enters the storm drain system.

If you choose to replant your swale, select a time when heavy downpours are uncommon. For many areas of the country, this time falls during the late summer and early autumn. This is especially true if you are seeding with a native grass/wildflower mix. A heavy rain may well wash the seeds away before they can set roots.

Always keep seeded areas moist during germination and make sure to protect bare soil with an erosion control blanket. Erosion control blankets are made of straw, coconut fiber, excelsior, or a combination of these materials and come in a variety of widths on a long roll. Spread the erosion blanket out over the area and peg it down to keep it in place. As the vegetation grows, the blanket will eventually disappear into the soil.

You can also plant a fast-growing, annual cover crop, such as oats or wheatgrass. These plants provide erosion control during the first season, giving the slower growing seedling a chance to take root. After one season, the cover crop dies and the perennial flowers and grasses take over.

A swale is the perfect spot to grow attractive, easy-to-care-for native plants. The deep roots do a great job of holding soil in place and preventing erosion. Once established, native plants are also a breeze to maintain. Imagine no more mowing or using the trimmer to keep the vegetation down in your swale.

OPPOSITE: Turning a roadside swale or ditch into a native wildflower planting improves water quality by slowing down and absorbing rainwater runoff.

PLANTING YOUR RAIN GARDEN

Once you've selected the proper place for your rain

garden and completed construction, the fun begins:

selecting plants and designing your garden.

Just because this is a functional part of your

landscape, it doesn't mean it can't be beautiful,

as well as a haven for desirable wildlife, such as

pollinating insects, butterflies, and songbirds.

Even though they serve an important purpose, rain gardens can still be attractive assets to a home landscape.

Creating a Plant List

When it comes to deciding what to plant, your main goal is to choose plants appropriate for your site that will take care of the necessary business of managing storm water. Within these requirements, you can also make choices based on wildlife attraction, season-long interest, bloom times, and even your favorite colors. Although most rain gardens are heavy on herbaceous perennial flowers, there are also many grasses and ferns that will thrive in these gardens. And in larger gardens, there are several shrubs and trees for consideration. The end result should be a functional garden that manages your rainwater, fits your desired level of maintenance, and still looks good in your yard and neighborhood.

One important thing to keep in mind when selecting plants: You are not looking for wetland or water garden plants or those that require very dry soil conditions. Rather, you are looking for plants that can tolerate saturated soil for a period of time but are also able to withstand drought conditions, especially in the central part of the garden. As you move toward the outsides of the garden, you can incorporate more traditional garden and landscape plants.

There are several other factors to keep in mind when creating your plant list. Some of them are practical, such as selecting plants that will survive your winter temperatures and will grow well in your available sunlight. Others are more subjective, such as flower color, seasonal interest, and attraction to birds and butterflies. We'll start with the more practical issues and work our way down the list.

A leafhopper lays its eggs on a coneflower stem. By selecting a variety of plants for your rain garden, you can create habitat for a variety of creatures.

"Oxeye" is a common name for this native rain garden plant (*Heliopsis helianthoides*), on left, as well as for an unrelated perennial native to Europe (*Leucanthemum vulgare*), on right, that can become invasive. A good reason why you can't always rely on common names! *Right image ©Shutterstock.com*

Plant Names

One of the most confusing things about selecting plants is understanding the lingo. You may feel as though you need to learn a whole new language before you can successfully shop for a plant! Here are a few terms that will be helpful to know as you walk the aisles of a garden center or peruse the pages of a nursery catalog.

Common names are given to plants by the people who use them. Although they are fun and popular, they can be confusing because they often differ in different areas of the country and several plants may share the same common name.

A better name to learn is the **botanical name**, which consists of two parts: genus and species. This name is Latin, which can make for some interesting pronunciations, but each plant has only one correct botanical name, and if you use this name (even if you pronounce it incorrectly!), you can be assured of just what plant you are getting.

The first part of the two-part botanical name is the **genus**. It indicates a group of plants with similar characteristics, usually flowering and fruiting parts. It is followed by the **species**, which more specifically describes the individual plant. The genus name is capitalized and is followed by the lowercased species name. The two words are usually set in italics or underlined, as compared to the common name, which is not.

A **cultivar** ("cultivated variety") is a plant set apart because it has one or more traits that distinguish it from the species. It does not occur naturally but rather is maintained by cultivation. A cultivar name should be placed in single quotes and placed behind the species name or before the common name, but it is not always found this way. Sometimes it is used alone and sometimes it is used as a common name. And sometimes it is indicated by a "cv." in front of it.

A **hybrid** is a plant that originated from a cross between two species. It is set off by a small *x* before the species name. Hybrids are plants that have been manipulated to have the best qualities of each parent. You can have a cultivar of a hybrid.

Other names gardeners may run across include **patent** and **trademark** names. These are similar to common names, but they are patented by the breeder and cannot be used for any other plants. These names are indicated by the symbols ™ or ® and they are not set in single quotes.

Annuals complete their life cycle in one growing season, usually starting out as seeds in spring and die when a frost hits or they have set seeds and completed their "mission" on this earth. They may reseed, but generally annuals are replanted every year. Examples of annuals include petunia, marigold, lettuce, and carrot.

Perennials live for more than one growing season, if all goes well, that is! These plants have root systems that survive winters. This term is generally used to describe herbaceous plants, but technically it applies to woody plants as well. Herbaceous perennials have a shorter blooming period than annuals, but they live from year to year. Examples of perennials include hostas, asters, and goldenrods.

Biennials require two growing seasons to complete their life cycle. Typically they grow leaves the first year and then produce flowers the second season. Examples of biennials include foxglove, hollyhock, and sweet William. They are typically sold as second-year plants that will bloom the year you buy them and are often grouped with annuals.

Herbaceous plants are those that have soft, succulent, non-woody stems. Annuals, perennials, bulbs, and grasses are herbaceous. They are in contrast to **woody plants**, which have bark or some other hard tissue that persists from year to year. Woody plants include trees, shrubs, and vines, which all grow in diameter from year to year.

Plants can be **evergreen** or **deciduous**. Deciduous plants lose all their leaves at one point, usually in fall, and get a new set, usually in spring. Evergreen plants have leaves that stay green and growing throughout the year. They are typically thought of as needled conifers like spruces and pines, but there are also "broad-leaved" evergreen plants, such as rhododendrons. Some herbaceous plants also remain evergreen throughout the year. All evergreens have their leaves replaced, but because it is not all at once like deciduous plants, it is less noticeable.

Dioecious and **monoecious** are terms used to describe where a plant's reproductive parts are found. Plants that have male and female flowers on separate plants are dioecious. Plants that have both flower types on the same plant are monoecious. This is mainly important if you are growing plants that you either want to produce fruits or you don't want to produce fruits. If you want fruits on dioecious plants (e.g., hollies), you need to make sure you plant both male and female plants. If you don't want fruits (e.g., gingko) you want to make sure you only plant a male species.

ABOVE: This plant can be correctly called any of the following: red maple, rock maple, scarlet maple, soft maple, swamp maple, or water maple (common names) *Acer rubrum* (species name); 'Franksred' (cultivar name); or Red Sunset™ (trademark name).

LEFT: 'Goldsturm' is a common cultivar of black-eyed Susan (*Rudbeckia fulgida*). It is good for gardeners to know cultivar names, since this is how many plants are labeled at garden centers.

Winter Hardiness

Hardiness zones indicate the severity of winter temperatures. The lower the number, the more severe the winter climate. This book uses the most common system—the United States Department of Agriculture (USDA) Hardiness Zones—a system based on average annual minimum winter temperatures. You can locate your hardiness zone on the map on page 186. While it is important to know your hardiness zone and choose plants that will survive in your zone, don't live and die by it. Use it as a guideline. A plant's ability to survive winter is affected by many factors, such as snow cover, soil moisture, the plant's age, and winter mulching.

Available Sunlight

Obviously you will need to choose plants that tolerate your available sunlight. If possible, observe your rain garden site at various times of the growing season to determine your available sunlight and then choose plants appropriate for the amount of light your garden gets. Keep in mind that if your garden is large, you may have varying sunlight levels within it. And remember that you do have some control over available light. You can prune the lower limbs of some nearby trees to increase the amount of sunlight your garden receives.

The degrees of sunlight and shade range from full sun to light or partial shade to heavy shade and are different at different times of the growing season. "Full sun" is found in areas with no overhead obstructions where plants will receive six hours or more of direct sun. "Light shade" areas receive bright to full sun for all but a few hours each day. There may be a partial canopy of trees overhead, but it does not shade the area for very long. Areas with bright light or sun for about half the day are called "partial shade" or "medium shade." Most shade plants will do fine in either light or partial shade, especially if the sun is morning sun. "Full shade," also called "dense shade," areas are shaded for most of the day, often under a full canopy of trees, and are suitable for only the most shade-tolerant plants.

Wild geranium (*Geranium maculatum*) and foamflower (*Tiarella cordifolia*) are good choices for shady rain gardens.

Plants Organized by Sunlight Requirements

FULL SUN

Perennials

Achillea 'Moonshine' (moonshine yarrow)

Allium cernuum (nodding wild onion)

Amsonia tabernaemontana (eastern bluestar)

Aquilegia species (columbines)

Asclepias incarnata (swamp milkweed)

Asclepias tuberosa (butterfly milkweed)

Baptisia species (wild indigos)

Boltonia asteroides (doll's daisy)

Chelone species (turtleheads)

Coreopsis species (tickseeds)

Echinacea purpurea (purple coneflower)

Eupatoriadelphus species (Joe pye weeds)

Filipendula rubra (queen of the prairie)

Gentiana species (gentians)

Helenium autumnale (sneezeweed)

Heliopsis helianthoides (oxeye)

Hibiscus moscheutos (common rose mallow)

Iris species (iris, blue flags)

Liatris species (blazing stars)

Lilium michiganense (Michigan lily)

Lobelia species (cardinal flower, blue lobelia)

Monarda species (bee balm, wild bergamot)

Penstemon digitalis (foxglove beardtongue)

Phlox glaberrima (smooth phlox)

Phlox maculata (meadow phlox)

Phlox pilosa (prairie phlox)

Phlox stolonifera (creeping phlox)

Physostegia virginiana (obedient plant)

Ratibida pinnata (gray-headed coneflower)

Rudbeckia species (black-eyed Susans)

Ruellia humilis (wild petunia)

Silphium species (silphiums)

Solidago species (goldenrods)

Symphyotrichum species (asters)

Tradescantia ohiensis (spiderwort)

Vernonia species (ironweeds)

Veronicastrum virginicum (Culver's root)

Zizia aurea (golden alexanders)

Tickseed

Bee balm

Golden alexanders

Common rush

'Regent' serviceberry

Viburnum

Grasses

Andropogon gerardii (big bluestem)

Chasmanthium latifolium (northern sea oats)

Deschampsia caespitosa (tufted hairgrass)

Helictotrichon sempervirens (blue oat grass)

Juncus effusus (common rush)

Panicum virgatum (switchgrass)

Schizachyrium scoparium (little bluestem)

Sorghastrum nutans (Indian grass)

Shrubs and Trees

Acer rubrum (red maple)

Amelanchier species (serviceberries)

Betula nigra (river birch)

Carpinus caroliniana (American hornbeam)

Celtis occidentalis (hackberry)

Cephalanthus occidentalis (buttonbush)

Cercis canadensis (eastern redbud)

Clethra alnifolia (summersweet)

Cornus species (dogwoods)

Hamamelis species (witchhazels)

Ilex species (winterberry, hollies)

Itea virginica (Virginia sweetspire)

Lindera benzoin (spicebush)

Myrica (bayberries)

Nyssa sylvatica (black gum)

Photinia species (chokeberries)

Physocarpus species (ninebarks)

Quercus species (oaks)

Taxodium distichum (bald cypress)

Thuja occidentalis (arborvitae)

Vaccinium species (blueberries)

Viburnum species (viburnums)

PARTIAL TO FULL SHADE

Perennials

Actaea racemosa (bugbane)

Adiantum pedatum (maidenhair fern)

Anemone canadensis (Canadian anemone)

Aquilegia species (columbines)

Aruncus dioicus (goat's beard)

Asarum canadense (wild ginger)

Athyrium filix-femina (lady fern)

Geranium maculatum (wild geranium)

Iris cristata (crested iris)

Lobelia cardinalis (cardinal flower)

Matteuccia struthiopteris (ostrich fern)

Mertensia virginica (Virginia bluebells)

Phlox divaricata (woodland phlox)

Polemonium reptans (Jacob's ladder)

Polygonatum species (Solomon's seals)

Tiarella cordifolia (foamflower)

Tradescantia virginiana (Virginia spiderwort)

Grasses

Carex species (sedges)

Deschampsia caespitosa (tufted hairgrass)

Shrubs and Trees

Acer circinatum (vine maple)

Carpinus caroliniana (American hornbeam)

Hydrangea species (hydrangeas)

Itea virginica (Virginia sweetspire)

Lindera benzoin (spicebush)

Bloody cranesbill

Solomon's seal

Sedge

85

Saturation Zones

Once you've determined which plants will survive your winters and do well in your available light conditions, it's time to think about choosing appropriate plants for each of your saturation zones. A well-designed rain garden will have several different soil moisture zones. Plants in the deepest part of the garden, Zone A, must be able to tolerate periodic or frequent standing or flowing water as well as seasonal dry spells. This is also where you will want to place taller plants, keeping in mind that they will appear a foot or so shorter because this area of the garden is usually lower than the outsides.

Plants for Zone B, generally found in the area right around Zone A, should be those that grow well in average soil moisture. They will need to be able to tolerate some standing water but not for very long. If your percolation test results show you have a high infiltration rate, you can consider using plants that like average soil conditions (Zone B plants) in the bottom as well (Zone A), since your garden will drain readily and not hold water for too long.

Zone C plants should be able to tolerate average to dry conditions. Zone C plants tend to be shorter plants, since this zone is usually found around the outside of the garden. But don't be afraid to include some taller, fine-textured plants in this zone also.

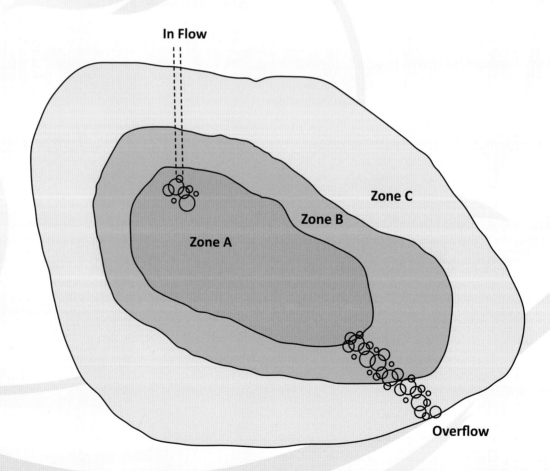

This drawing of a simple rain garden illustrates the three saturation zones along with typical inflow and overflow placement.

Plants Organized by Rain Garden Zone

ZONE A

Perennials

Actaea racemosa (bugbane)
Asclepias incarnata (swamp milkweed)
Athyrium filix-femina (lady fern)
Boltonia asteroides (doll's daisy)
Chelone species (turtleheads)
Coreopsis tripteris (tall tickseed)
Eupatoriadelphus species (Joe pye weeds)
Filipendula rubra (queen of the prairie)
Gentiana species (gentians)
Helenium autumnale (sneezeweed)
Heliopsis helianthoides (oxeye)
Hibiscus moscheutos (common rose mallow)
Iris species (iris, blue flags)
Liatris ligulistylis (Rocky Mountain blazing star)
Liatris pycnostachya (prairie blazing star)
Liatris spicata (dense blazing star)
Lilium michiganense (Michigan lily)
Lobelia species (cardinal flower, blue lobelia)
Matteuccia struthiopteris (ostrich fern)
Monarda didyma (bee balm)
Monarda fistulosa (wild bergamot)
Physostegia virginiana (obedient plant)
Rudbeckia fulgida (black-eyed Susan)
Rudbeckia hirta (black-eyed Susan)
Rudbeckia laciniata (cutleaf coneflower)
Rudbeckia subtomentosa (sweet coneflower)
Rudbeckia triloba (brown-eyed Susan)
Silphium species (silphiums)
Symphyotrichum novae-angliae (New England aster)
Tradescantia species (spiderworts)
Veronicastrum virginicum (Culver's root)

Queen of the prairie

Oxeye

Black-eyed Susan

Cup plant

Sedge

Grasses

Andropogon gerardii (big bluestem)

Carex species (sedges)

Chasmanthium latifolium (northern sea oats)

Juncus effusus (common rush)

Panicum virgatum (switchgrass)

Shrubs and Trees

Acer rubrum (red maple)

Amelanchier species (serviceberries)

Betula nigra (river birch)

Celtis occidentalis (hackberry)

Cephalanthus occidentalis (buttonbush)

Clethra alnifolia (summersweet)

Cornus species (dogwoods)

Ilex species (winterberry, hollies)

Itea virginica (Virginia sweetspire)

Nyssa sylvatica (black gum)

Photinia species (chokeberries)

Quercus species (oaks)

Taxodium distichum (bald cypress)

Thuja occidentalis (arborvitae)

Vaccinium corymbosum (highbush blueberry)

Viburnum species (viburnums)

ZONE B

Perennials

Achillea 'Moonshine' (moonshine yarrow)

Adiantum pedatum (maidenhair fern)

Amsonia tabernaemontana (eastern bluestar)

Anemone canadensis (Canadian anemone)

Aquilegia species (columbines)

Aruncus dioicus (goat's beard)

Asclepias tuberosa (butterfly milkweed)

Athyrium filix-femina (lady fern)

Baptisia species (wild indigos)

Chelone species (turtleheads)

Coreopsis verticillata (threadleaf tickseed, whorled tickseed)

Echinacea purpurea (purple coneflower)

Geranium maculatum (wild geranium)

Heliopsis helianthoides (oxeye)

Liatris aspera (rough blazing star)

Liatris spicata (dense blazing star)

Liatris squarrosa (scaly blazing star)

Lobelia siphilitica (blue lobelia)

Matteuccia struthiopteris (ostrich fern)

Mertensia virginica (Virginia bluebells)

Monarda bradburiana (eastern bee balm)

Monarda didyma (bee balm)

Monarda fistulosa (wild bergamot)

Penstemon digitalis (foxglove beardtongue)

Phlox divaricata (woodland phlox)

Phlox glaberrima (smooth phlox)

Phlox maculata (meadow phlox)

Physostegia virginiana (obedient plant)

Polygonatum species (Solomon's seals)

Ratibida pinnata (gray-headed coneflower)

Rudbeckia fulgida (black-eyed Susan)

Rudbeckia triloba (brown-eyed Susan)

Silphium species (silphiums)

Solidago species (goldenrods)

Symphyotrichum species (asters)

Tradescantia species (spiderworts)

Vernonia species (ironweeds)

Zizia aurea (golden alexanders)

Maidenhair fern

Wild indigo

'May Night' woodland phlox

Little bluestem

Eastern redbud

Grasses

Andropogon gerardii (big bluestem)

Chasmanthium latifolium (northern sea oats)

Deschampsia caespitosa (tufted hairgrass)

Panicum virgatum (switchgrass)

Schizachyrium scoparium (little bluestem)

Sorghastrum nutans (Indian grass)

Shrubs and Trees

Acer species (maples)

Amelanchier species (serviceberries)

Betula nigra (river birch)

Carpinus caroliniana (American hornbeam)

Celtis occidentalis (hackberry)

Cephalanthus occidentalis (buttonbush)

Cercis canadensis (eastern redbud)

Clethra alnifolia (summersweet)

Cornus species (dogwoods)

Hamamelis species (witchhazels)

Hydrangea species (hydrangeas)

Ilex species (winterberry, hollies)

Itea virginica (Virginia sweetspire)

Lindera benzoin (spicebush)

Myrica (bayberries)

Nyssa sylvatica (black gum)

Photinia species (chokeberries)

Physocarpus species (ninebarks)

Quercus species (oaks)

Thuja occidentalis (arborvitae)

Viburnum species (viburnums)

Butterfly milkweed

Woodland phlox

Ohio spiderwort

ZONE C

Perennials
Achillea 'Moonshine' (moonshine yarrow)
Allium cernuum (nodding wild onion)
Aquilegia species (columbines)
Asarum canadense (wild ginger)
Asclepias tuberosa (butterfly milkweed)
Iris cristata (crested iris)
Liatris squarrosa (scaly blazing star)
Mertensia virginica (Virginia bluebells)
Monarda bradburiana (eastern bee balm)
Penstemon digitalis (foxglove beardtongue)
Phlox divaricata (woodland phlox)
Phlox pilosa (prairie phlox)
Phlox stolonifera (creeping phlox)
Polemonium reptans (Jacob's ladder)
Ruellia humilis (wild petunia)
Tiarella cordifolia (foamflower)
Tradescantia species (spiderworts)
Zizia aurea (golden alexanders)

Grasses
Carex pensylvanica (Pennsylvania sedge)
Helictotrichon sempervirens (blue oat grass)
Schizachyrium scoparium (little bluestem)

91

Beyond Flowers

Most rain gardens are made up of herbaceous flowering plants, mainly perennials. However, don't discount the beauty, year-long interest, and wildlife value that grasses, ferns, and woody plants will bring to a rain garden.

Grasses provide interesting contrast to flowering plants and bring a lot of late summer, fall, and winter interest. Many provide food and shelter for birds and natural support for flowering plants, reducing the need for artificial staking. Grasses, sedges, and rushes also create a thick underground network of roots that helps stabilize the soil, keeps plants from moving around too much, and deters weeds. Ferns are good additions to shady rain gardens, providing nice contrast to flowering plants. And they fill in nicely after the main spring show in shade gardens.

Larger rain gardens can also include shrubs, small trees, and even large shade trees. They just need to fit the requirements of your site and the saturation zone you want to use them in.

A good tree to start with is an oak. Not only are oaks beautiful, but they are long-lived and they support more species of butterflies, and thus bird food, than any other plant. Unfortunately many species are just too big for urban situations and not all species do well in rain garden zone A. Two that do are swamp white oak and pin oak. Other good native trees to consider for larger sites are red maple and river birch.

BELOW LEFT: Grasses not only add interest to rain gardens, they also help stabilize the soil and provide support for flowers.

BELOW RIGHT: If you have the room, oaks are great choices for rain gardens.

'Princess Diana' apple serviceberry (*Amelanchier x grandiflora*) is a nice small tree that does well in rain gardens.

Most landscapes require smaller trees that are in better scale in city and suburban settings and won't threaten overhead power lines and create problems of too much shade as they get older. Good small trees for use in rain gardens include apple serviceberry, hop hornbeam, and arborvitae cultivars.

There are several shrubs that do well in rain gardens. However, be aware that many of them are suckering shrubs and are best used in larger rain gardens where they can be allowed to expand somewhat. Shrubs that are suitable for rain gardens include serviceberries, hydrangeas, chokeberries, ninebark cultivars, and viburnums.

For detailed information on plants to consider using in your rain garden, see the Plant Index section of this book.

'Dayspring' oakleaf hydrangea (*Hydrangea quercifolia*) is a good shrub for rain gardens.

Gray-headed coneflower (*Ratibida pinnata*), wild bergamot (*Monarda fistulosa*), and anise hyssop (*Agastache foeniculum*) are all good native plants for rain gardens.

Using Native Plants

By installing a rain garden on your property you are doing a great benefit to the environment. It just makes sense to take it one step further and use native plants whenever practical. Fortunately, many native plants are great choices for the conditions found in rain gardens.

Native plants are those species that grew naturally in an area before the greatest influx of European settlement, about the mid-1800s in most areas of the country. Unlike most introduced plants, a native plant fully integrates itself into a biotic community, establishing complex relationships with other local plants and animals. Not only does a native plant depend on the organisms with which it has evolved, but the other organisms also depend on it, creating a true web of life. This natural system of checks and balances ensures that native plants seldom grow out of control in their natural habitats.

"Wildflower" is a commonly used term, but it does not necessarily mean a native plant, since not all wildflowers are native to an area. Wildflowers include introduced plants that have escaped cultivation and grow wild in areas. Examples are Queen Anne's lace (*Daucus carota*) and chicory (*Chicorium intybus*), two common roadside plants, neither of which is native to any area of the United States.

Native prairie species, especially those that evolved in seasonally moist prairies, are especially well suited to rain gardens. Most of them have deep root systems that will help them survive summer dry spells. These extensive root systems also create natural channels that help keep the soil loose and improve infiltration.

There are many additional benefits to using native plants in rain gardens, as well as other areas of your landscape. For many gardeners, the initial attraction comes from native plants' reputation of being lower maintenance than a manicured lawn and exotic shrubs. For the most part this is true—provided native plants are given landscape situations that match their cultural requirements. Because they have evolved and adapted to their surroundings, native plants tend to be tolerant of tough conditions like drought and poor soil. Native plants are better adapted to local climatic conditions and better able to resist the effects of native insects and diseases.

The less tangible—but possibly more important—side of using native plants, is the connection you make with nature. Gardening with natives instills an understanding of our natural world—its cycles, changes, and history. By observing native plants throughout the year, a gardener gains insight into seasonal rhythms and life cycles. You will see an increase in wildlife, including birds, butterflies, and pollinating insects, making your garden a livelier place.

On a broader scale, using native plants helps preserve the natural heritage of an area. Genetic diversity promotes the mixing of genes to form new combinations, the key to adaptability and survival of all life. Once a species becomes extinct, it is gone forever, as are its genes and any future contribution that it might have made. Choosing plants that have evolved in conditions similar to your planting site not only helps ensure greater success for you, it also serves local pollinators and other wildlife and helps preserve genetic diversity within a species. As we lose more and more of our natural areas, landscape plantings become important refuges for our native insects and other wildlife.

Despite the increased interest in and promotion of native plants, many people still hesitate to use them for one reason or another. Some of the common misconceptions about using native plants are that they are colorless and dull, sources of allergy-causing pollen, invasive, hard to grow, messy, and hard to locate in the nursery trade. Hopefully with a little education about the wide variety of native plants available and how to use them properly, you will find that all of these myths can be dispelled.

As beneficial as they might be, there are certain native species that are just too coarse and unrefined to be used in traditional landscape settings. There are a lot of improved cultivars that are better behaved, and these are still usually better choices than resorting to over-used exotic species that can invade natural habitats. New England aster is a good example. This is a great plant for rain gardens, tolerating wet feet and providing beautiful purple flowers in the fall that butterflies love. But the species can grow quite tall and the lower leaves tend to turn brown by midsummer. There are several dwarf cultivars of New England aster—including 'Purple Dome,' which usually stays under two feet tall—that are usually better suited to traditional landscape use.

ABOVE: 'Miss Manners' is a less aggressive selection of obedient plant (*Physostegia virginiana*) that can be considered in smaller rain gardens.

Root System Depths and Heights

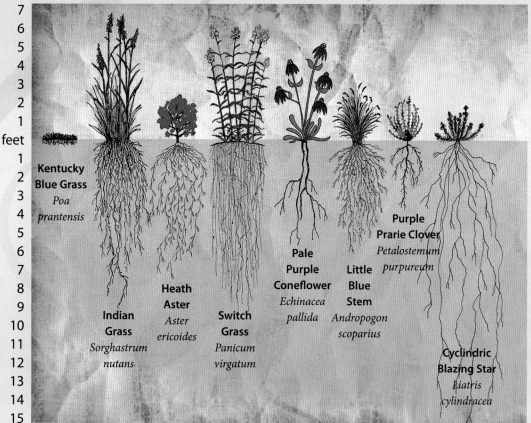

7
6
5
4
3
2
1
feet
1
2
3
4
5
6
7
8
9
10
11
12
13
14
15

Kentucky Blue Grass *Poa prantensis*

Indian Grass *Sorghastrum nutans*

Heath Aster *Aster ericoides*

Switch Grass *Panicum virgatum*

Pale Purple Coneflower *Echinacea pallida*

Little Blue Stem *Andropogon scoparius*

Purple Prarie Clover *Petalostemum purpureum*

Cyclindric Blazing Star *Liatris cylindracea*

This drawing shows how extensive native prairie plant roots are in comparison with Kentucky bluegrass. © *Jeffrey C. Domm*

Virginia bluebells (*Mertensia virginica*) bring a bright splash of color to rain gardens in spring.

Year-Round Interest

As functional as it is, your rain garden can still be a place to experiment with colors and textures, combining plants that not only grow well together, but also complement each other. With a little thought about what plants to use and how to place them, you can end up with a showy border that provides landscape interest all year long.

Most of the recommended rain garden plants are showiest from midsummer into late fall, so it's easy to have a showy garden in summer. The trick is to have something in bloom throughout the growing season, from early spring until the snow falls and even through the winter. Incorporate spring bloomers like Jacob's ladder, bluestars, geraniums, and Virginia bluebells to detract from the brown hummocks of the grasses. Fall bloomers, such as asters and sneezeweed, are showy late in the season and most grasses turn beautiful shades of red

and copper in fall and hold their color well into winter. Chokecherries, hydrangeas, maples, and sumacs are just some of the woody plants that are showy in fall.

But even the best-planned garden will have color gaps. Place an emphasis on choosing plants with interesting foliage shapes and textures, since foliage is usually decorative for much longer than flowers are. Incorporate a variety of foliage colors, including traditional greens in all shades, silvers, blues, chartreuse, and the occasional variegated form. Good foliage plants include bugbane, heucheras, ferns, wild ginger, wild indigos, Solomon's seal, and foamflower.

A rain garden doesn't have to get all its color from flowers. Foliage plants like *Heuchera* 'Green Spice' offer interest throughout the growing season.

Highbush cranberry (*Viburnum trilobum*) adds a lot of fall and winter interest with its showy foliage and persistent fruits.

Evergreens are essential to winter landscapes, not only for the color they offer but also for providing a backdrop for showy seed heads of grasses. But many other woody ornaments offer interesting bark and seedpods and colorful fruits that persist through winter. Red-twigged dogwood has showy red stems in winter that are especially attractive against a snowy backdrop. Hollies and viburnums are among the shrubs that have showy persistent fruits.

Many herbaceous plants can also provide interest into winter. Allow goldenrods, wild onions, purple coneflowers, and Joe pye weeds to remain through the winter so their dried flower heads can provide visual interest as well as food for birds. Plants with showy persistent fruits and seedpods include wild indigoes, milkweeds, and Solomon's seal.

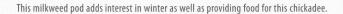

This milkweed pod adds interest in winter as well as providing food for this chickadee.

Canada columbine

Foamflower

Plants with Seasonal Interest

SPRING

Perennials

Amsonia tabernaemontana (eastern bluestar)
Anemone canadensis (Canadian anemone)
Aquilegia species (columbines)
Aruncus dioicus (goat's beard)
Asarum canadense (wild ginger)
Baptisia species (wild indigos)
Geranium maculatum (wild geranium)
Iris species (iris, blue flags)
Matteuccia struthiopteris (ostrich fern)
Mertensia virginica (Virginia bluebells)
Phlox species (phloxes)
Polemonium reptans (Jacob's ladder)
Tiarella cordifolia (foamflower)
Zizia aurea (golden alexanders)

Grasses

Carex pensylvanica (Pennsylvania sedge)
Deschampsia caespitosa (tufted hairgrass)
Helictotrichon sempervirens (blue oat grass)

Shrubs and Trees

Amelanchier species (serviceberries)
Cercis canadensis (eastern redbud)
Hamamelis vernalis species (spring witchhazel)
Lindera benzoin (spicebush)
Viburnum species (viburnums)

Nodding wild onion

Sneezeweed

Little bluestem

FALL

Perennials

Allium cernuum (nodding wild onion)
Asarum canadense (wild ginger)
Athyrium filix-femina (lady fern)
Baptisia species (wild indigos)
Boltonia asteroides (doll's daisy)
Chelone species (turtleheads)
Echinacea purpurea (purple coneflower)
Eupatoriadelphus species (Joe pye weeds)
Gentiana species (gentians)
Geranium maculatum (wild geranium)
Helenium autumnale (sneezeweed)
Physostegia virginiana (obedient plant)
Polygonatum species (Solomon's seals)
Rudbeckia species (black eyed Susans)
Symphyotrichum species (asters)
Tiarella cordifolia (foamflower)

Grasses

Andropogon gerardii (big bluestem)
Chasmanthium latifolium (northern sea oats)
Deschampsia caespitosa (tufted hairgrass)
Helictotrichon sempervirens (blue oat grass)
Juncus effusus (common rush)
Panicum virgatum (switchgrass)
Schizachyrium scoparium (little bluestem)
Sorghastrum nutans (Indian grass)

Shrubs and Trees

Acer species (maples)
Amelanchier species (serviceberries)
Carpinus caroliniana (American hornbeam)
Clethra alnifolia (summersweet)
Cornus species (dogwoods)
Hamamelis virginiana (witchhazel)
Hydrangea quercifolia (oakleaf hydrangea)
Ilex species (winterberry, hollies)
Itea virginica (Virginia sweetspire)
Lindera benzoin (spicebush)
Nyssa sylvatica (black gum)
Photinia species (chokeberries)
Taxodium distichum (bald cypress)
Vaccinium species (blueberries)
Viburnum species (viburnums)

Joe pye weed and coneflower

Arborvitae. ©Shutterstock.com

WINTER

Perennials

Allium cernuum (nodding wild onion)

Baptisia species (wild indigos)

Echinacea purpurea (purple coneflower)

Rudbeckia species (black-eyed Susans)

Grasses

Andropogon gerardii (big bluestem)

Chasmanthium latifolium (northern sea oats)

Deschampsia caespitosa (tufted hairgrass)

Juncus effusus (common rush)

Panicum virgatum (switchgrass)

Schizachyrium scoparium (little bluestem)

Sorghastrum nutans (Indian grass)

Shrubs and Trees

Amelanchier species (serviceberries)

Carpinus caroliniana (American hornbeam)

Cercis canadensis (eastern redbud)

Clethra alnifolia (summersweet)

Cornus sericea (red-osier dogwood)

Ilex species (winterberry, hollies)

Thuja occidentalis (arborvitae)

Viburnum species (viburnums)

A variety of plant heights adds to the visual appeal of a rain garden.

Plant Height

Most gardeners will want to include a range of plant heights to help keep things interesting. Remember that many factors can affect plant height, including available sunlight, soil moisture, and fertility levels. Also keep in mind that plants in the middle of the rain garden will often appear up to a foot shorter because they are planted in a lower area of the garden.

One drawback of using tall plants is their need for staking. Growing shrubs or tall grasses nearby can provide some natural support if you want to avoid the maintenance issue of staking. You can cut them back in late spring to reduce their heights and also stagger bloom time. This technique is explained in Chapter 4.

Joe pye weed

Cardinal flower

Culver's root

Perennials and Grasses by Height

TALL (OVER 3 FEET)

Actaea racemosa (bugbane)
Aruncus dioicus (goat's beard)
Asclepias incarnata (swamp milkweed)
Baptisia australis (blue wild indigo)
Boltonia asteroides (doll's daisy)
Chelone species (turtleheads)
Coreopsis tripteris (tall tickseed)
Echinacea purpurea (purple coneflower)
Eupatoriadelphus species (Joe pye weeds)
Filipendula rubra (queen of the prairie)
Helenium autumnale (sneezeweed)
Heliopsis helianthoides (oxeye)
Hibiscus moscheutos (common rose mallow)
Iris species (iris, blue flags)
Liatris aspera (rough blazing star)
Liatris ligulistylis (Rocky Mountain blazing star)
Liatris pycnostachya (prairie blazing star)
Lilium michiganense (Michigan lily)
Lobelia cardinalis (cardinal flower)
Matteuccia struthiopteris (ostrich fern)
Monarda didyma (bee balm)
Monarda fistulosa (wild bergamot)
Ratibida pinnata (gray-headed coneflower)
Rudbeckia laciniata(cutleaf coneflower)
Rudbeckia subtomentosa (sweet coneflower)
Rudbeckia triloba (brown-eyed Susan)
Silphium species (silphiums)
Solidago species (goldenrods)
Symphyotrichum novae-angliae (New England aster)
Vernonia species (ironweeds)
Veronicastrum virginicum (Culver's root)

Grasses

Andropogon gerardii (big bluestem)
Chasmanthium latifolium (northern sea oats)
Deschampsia caespitosa (tufted hairgrass)
Panicum virgatum (switchgrass)
Sorghastrum nutans (Indian grass)

MEDIUM (1 TO 3 FEET)

Achillea 'Moonshine' (moonshine yarrow)
Adiantum pedatum (maidenhair fern)
Allium cernuum (nodding wild onion)
Amsonia tabernaemontana (eastern bluestar)
Anemone canadensis (Canadian anemone)
Aquilegia species (columbines)
Asclepias tuberosa (butterfly milkweed)
Athyrium filix-femina (lady fern)
Baptisia australis var. *minor* (blue wild indigo)
Baptisia sphaerocarpa (yellow wild indigo)
Coreopsis species (tickseeds)
Gentiana species (gentians)
Geranium maculatum (wild geranium)
Liatris spicata (dense blazing star)
Liatris squarrosa (scaly blazing star)
Lobelia siphilitica (blue lobelia)
Mertensia virginica (Virginia bluebells)
Monarda bradburiana (eastern bee balm)
Penstemon digitalis (foxglove beardtongue)
Phlox glaberrima (smooth phlox)
Phlox maculata (meadow phlox)
Phlox pilosa (prairie phlox)
Physostegia virginiana (obedient plant)
Polygonatum species (Solomon's seals)
Rudbeckia fulgida (black-eyed Susan)
Rudbeckia hirta (black-eyed Susan)
Ruellia humilis (wild petunia)
Solidago species (goldenrods)
Symphyotrichum species (asters)
Tradescantia species (spiderworts)
Zizia aurea (golden alexanders)

Grasses

Carex species (sedges)
Helictotrichon sempervirens (blue oat grass)
Schizachyrium scoparium (little bluestem)

SHORT (UNDER 1 FOOT)

Asarum canadense (wild ginger)
Iris cristata (crested iris)
Phlox divaricata (woodland phlox)
Phlox stolonifera (creeping phlox)
Polemonium reptans (Jacob's ladder)
Tiarella cordifolia (foamflower)

Grasses

Carex pensylvanica (Pennsylvania sedge)

Nodding wild onion

Dense blazing star

Prairie phlox

Goldenrod

Joe pye weed (*Eupatoriadelphus*) is good for attracting swallowtails and other butterflies.

Attraction to Wildlife

As much as you will get from your rain garden, the benefit to native fauna will be even greater, providing food and shelter necessary for their survival in a world where their natural habitats are quickly being destroyed. Even a small rain garden can have great benefits for insects and in turn birds and other wildlife further up the food chain. Beneficial insects prefer a less-manicured landscape, so a rain garden is a natural attraction for them. If you'd like your rain garden to serve double duty and provide habitat for birds, butterflies, pollinating insects, and other wildlife, you'll want to put more emphasis on choosing plants that are higher in wildlife value.

Many of the recommended flowers are natural havens for everyone's favorite insects, butterflies, which love open sunny habitats often found in rain gardens. Most butterflies are vagabonds on their way to somewhere else when you see them in your garden. You can think of your garden as a rest stop along the way, a place where they can linger for a while to enjoy food, water, and shelter. Make sure you have plants available during all of the growing season, from spring when butterflies first arrive to late fall. Early blooming prairie violets are occasionally weighted down with butterflies, as are late-blooming asters and Joe pye weeds. Including shrubs, trees, and bushy flowers will provide butterflies with shelter where they can hide from birds, find shade at midday, and rest at night.

Butterfly milkweed

Michigan lily

Purple coneflower

Plants to Attract Butterflies and Their Caterpillars

If you want to provide a complete butterfly habitat you will have to include the proper host plants for butterflies to lay eggs, keeping in mind that these are not always the showiest plants and that they become even less attractive when they have been eaten by the newly hatched caterpillars. These host plants are important, however, since without them butterflies will not lay eggs.

Achillea 'Moonshine' (moonshine yarrow)

Allium cernuum (nodding onion)

Amelanchier species (serviceberries)

Amsonia species (bluestars)

Andropogon gerardii (big bluestem)

Asclepias species (milkweeds)

Baptisia species (wild indigos)

Betula nigra (river birch)

Boltonia asteroides (doll's daisy)

Carex pensylvanica (Pennsylvania sedge)

Carpinus caroliniana (American hornbeam)

Celtis occidentalis (hackberry)

Cephalanthus occidentalis (buttonbush)

Cercis canadensis (eastern redbud)

Chelone species (turtleheads)

Clethra alnifolia (summersweet)

Coreopsis species (tickseeds)

Dalea purpurea (purple prairie clover)

Deschampsia caespitosa (tufted hairgrass)

Echinacea purpurea (purple coneflower)

Eupatoriadelphus species (Joe pye weeds)

Helenium autumnale (autumn sneezeweed)

Heliopsis helianthoides (oxeye)

Iris species (iris, blue flags)

Itea virginica (Virginia sweetspire)

Liatris species (blazing stars)

Lilium michiganense (Michigan lily)

Lindera benzoin (spicebush)

Lobelia species (cardinal flower, blue lobelia)

Monarda species (bee balm, wild bergamot)

Panicum virgatum (switchgrass)

Penstemon digitalis (foxglove beardtongue)

Phlox species (phloxes)

Quercus species (oaks)

Ironweed

Ratibida pinnata (gray-headed coneflower)

Rudbeckia species (black-eyed Susan, coneflowers)

Schizachyrium scoparium (little bluestem)

Silphium species (silphiums)

Solidago species (goldenrods)

Sorghastrum nutans (Indiangrass)

Symphyotrichum species (asters)

Vaccinium species (blueberries)

Vernonia species (ironweeds)

Veronicastrum virginicum (Culver's root)

Viburnum species (viburnums)

Zizia aurea (golden alexanders)

Blazing stars (*Liatris* species) are monarch magnets in late summer rain gardens.

Studies show that even small native landscapes provide mini stopover refuges for migratory birds and help to compensate for the rapidly occurring loss of large expanses of natural habitats. Blazing stars, purple coneflowers, asters, black-eyed Susans, and goldenrods are important food sources for goldfinches and other seed-eating birds. But remember that most birds are insectivores. You want to be sure to have a diversity of plants to attract a diversity of insects, aka food, for birds. Ideally your rain garden will have nearby trees and shrubs for birds to nest in and where they can roost and find shelter from the elements. You can also supplement nesting sites by erecting nesting boxes.

Bluebell

Royal catchfly

Alumroot

Plants to Attract Hummingbirds

Hummingbirds are always a welcome sight. Most hummingbird-attracting flowers are tubular in shape and many are red, but certainly not all. If you are interested in attracting these feathered friends to your rain garden, consider adding some of these plants.

Aquilegia species (columbines)
Asclepias species (milkweeds)
Baptisia species (wild indigos)
Campanula rotundifolia (harebell)
Chelone species (turtleheads)
Dalea purpurea (purple prairie clover)
Echinacea purpurea (purple coneflower)
Gaillardia xgrandiflora (hybrid blanket flower)
Heliopsis helianthoides (oxeye)
Heuchera species (alumroots)
Liatris species (blazing stars)
Lilium species (lilies)
Lobelia cardinalis (cardinal flower)
Monarda species (bee balm, wild bergamot)
Penstemon digitalis (foxglove beardtongue)
Phlox species (phloxes)
Physostegia virginiana (obedient plant)
Ruellia humilis (wild petunia)
Silene regia (royal catchfly)
Silphium perfoliatum (cup plant)
Symphoricarpos albus (snowberry)
Symphyotrichum species (asters)
Thalictrum species (meadow rues)
Verbena hastata (blue vervain)

Cardinal flower

Salt Tolerance

Many rain gardens are built near roads where salt is applied in the winter. Road salt damages plants by interfering with water uptake, which can lead to browning and even death of some plants. If your soil is heavy and your garden is near a salted road, you will want to look for plants that can tolerate the salt. It may also be a good idea to stick with herbaceous plants that go dormant in winter rather than shrubs that are more easily damaged. If your soil is sandy and drains well, the road salt should flush through your soil before your plants start growing in spring.

Rain gardens planted next to salted roadways should include salt-tolerant perennials like butterfly milkweed (*Asclepias tuberosa*).

Switchgrass (*Panicum virgatum*), sedum (*Hylotelephium spectabile*), and hydrangeas (*Hydrangea* species) are all good choices for rain gardens that are planted along salted streets.

Plants that Tolerate Road Salt

Canada columbine

Perennials
Achillea species (yarrows)
Aquilegia species (columbines)
Asclepias tuberosa (butterfly weed)
Coreopsis verticillata (whorled tickseed)
Dianthus gratianopolitanus (cheddar pink)
Hemerocallis cultivars (daylilies)
Iris sibirica (Siberian iris)
Symphyotrichum species (asters)
Waldsteinia fragarioides (barren strawberry)

Grasses
Andropogon gerardii (big bluestem)
Chasmanthium latifolium (northern sea oats)
Helictotrichon sempervirens (blue oat grass)
Panicum virgatum (switchgrass)
Schizachyrium scoparium (little bluestem)

Shrubs and Trees
Celtis occidentalis (hackberry)
Clethra alnifolia (summersweet)
Cornus racemosa (gray dogwood)
Ginkgo biloba (ginkgo)
Gymnocladus dioicus (Kentucky coffeetree)
Hamamelis species (witchhazels)
Hydrangea species (hydrangeas)
Ilex species (winterberry, hollies)
Myrica (bayberries)
Nyssa sylvatica (black gum)
Philadelphus lewesii (Lewis' mock orange)
Photinia species (chokeberries)
Rhus species (sumacs)
Symphoricarpos species (snowberries)
Syringa reticulata (Japanese tree lilac)
Taxodium distichum (bald cypress)
Viburnum dentatum (arrowwood)

New England aster

Little bluestem

'Gro-Low' fragrant sumac

Northern oriole on riverbank grape (*Vitis riparia*).

Plants to Avoid

As was stated earlier in this chapter, you want to stay away from plants that require saturated soil or very dry soil throughout their growing season. They will not do well with the moisture fluctuations in your garden. If you want to include a plant that is not listed in the Plant Index section of this book, do your research to make sure it will be able to tolerate your soil conditions.

If your rain garden is small, you will probably want to avoid including prolific seeders and/or aggressive spreaders. (Plants with these tendencies are pointed out in the Plant Index.) While these traits may be acceptable, and even welcome, in larger rain gardens, these plants can become weedy in smaller gardens.

If you really want to include some of these more aggressive plants, there are some maintenance techniques you can use to keep these plants under control. With a little education, you can learn the seedling stages of these plants and be ready to weed some of them out or transplant them as soon as they reach a suitable size. You may also want to deadhead some of the more prolific seeders before they get a chance to set seed. Obviously this will reduce their value to seed-eating birds and mammals, but it may be a compromise that is worth considering in some cases. Spreading plants can be kept in check by digging out some of the encroaching stems and roots each spring.

Periwinkle (*Vinca minor*) is an example of a popular landscape plant that has become invasive in some areas of the country.

Most importantly, be sure to avoid any exotic invasive plants that can escape to nearby natural areas and become pests there by crowding out native species and thereby destroying ecosystems. After land clearing, the invasion of exotic plants is the second greatest threat to our natural areas.

If you want to use exotic plants in your rain garden, avoid planting those species that are known to have invaded local natural areas and caused habitat destruction. This list includes such familiar landscape plants as bugleweed (*Ajuga reptans*), baby's breath (*Gypsophila paniculata*), spotted deadnettle (*Lamium maculatum*), Amur maple (*Acer ginnala*), Norway maple (*Acer platanoides*), tree of heaven (*Ailanthus altissima*), barberries (*Berberis* species), Siberian peashrub (*Caragana arborescens*), burning bush (*Euonymus alatus*), common privet (*Ligustrum vulgare*), and European mountain ash (*Sorbus aucuparia*). For an up-to-date list of invasive plants in your region, refer to the Invasive Plant Atlas of the Unites States at www.invasiveplantatlas.org.

Obedient plant (*Physostegia virginiana*) is a beautiful plant but spreads aggressively and should be used with caution in small rain gardens.

A deer in the yard.
© Becky Sheridan/
Shutterstock.com

Resistance to Deer

If deer are a problem in your area (you are not alone!), you may want to consider selecting plants that are usually avoided by deer. A plant's resistance to deer feeding is affected by fluctuations in deer populations, availability of alternative food, the time of year, environmental factors, and even individual animal preference. No plant is safe under all conditions, but a list of rain garden plants that show up regularly on deer-resistant lists is on page 143.

Designing Your Garden

If you have given careful thought to plant selection and included plants that bloom at different times and have interesting foliage, bark, and fruits, you will ensure that there is something interesting going on year round in your rain garden. But you should also give careful thought to how the plants all work together to create a well-designed part of your overall landscape. These considerations are especially important if you are using nontraditional landscape plants like natives.

When it comes to acceptably incorporating native plants into traditional landscapes, the most important thing is to show intent rather than neglect. If you live in an urban area and need to be cognizant of what your neighbors and city officials think, or if you just prefer a more traditional, well-tended look, there are many things you can do to make your rain garden look less "wild." By incorporating traditional design principles and maintenance practices that illustrate that your landscape is cared for and intentional, you'll show people you haven't just allowed "weeds" to move in and take over.

Rain gardens in the front yard should be well designed and maintained.

If you want a traditional-looking landscape or are placing your rain garden in your front yard, you'll want to stick with plants with a more controllable growth habit. These tend to be clump-forming plants rather than spreaders. Clump-forming bunch grasses like little bluestem have a nice, neat, mounded form and are better choices for small landscapes than rhizomatous, spreading grasses. You'll probably also want to avoid using excessively tall plants; the front yard is probably not the place for cup plant or big bluestem grass.

Another way to help your landscape look more tended is to use traditional planting and design methods. Plant in groups of three, five, or seven plants as is more typical of nonnative landscapes rather than scattering them singly here and there. Limit your number of species and repeat a few specific plant groupings or color schemes at intervals throughout the garden. Include some areas of visual calm where the eye can rest momentarily from stimulation. A small grouping of silver-leaved plants or a simple green-leaved deciduous or evergreen shrub can create spots of calm.

There's no reason you can't incorporate ornaments into your rain garden, as long as they don't impede the flow of water. Sundials are nice additions to gardens in sunny spots. Birdbaths made of ceramic or stone are practical as well as beautiful. But don't be afraid to add anything that makes you happy and adds to your enjoyment of the space, including gazing balls, handmade decorations, wind chimes, and even pink flamingoes!

Birdbaths and other garden ornaments will add to the tended look of a rain garden.

Riparian Buffers

Does your property border a stream or other waterway? If it does, you can help protect the water quality by maintaining a riparian buffer zone along the water's edge. A riparian buffer is an area of dense, natural vegetation that borders a water body. The buffer does not have to be wide to be effective, usually ten to fifteen feet is wide enough.

Remember that rainwater running off your property may contain many things that harm water quality. Substances like motor oil from a spill on the driveway, over-applied pesticides and fertilizers, and even soil from bare spots on a lawn can degrade water and kill fish and other aquatic creatures. Passing through a simple border of vegetation before entering a stream or lake strips contaminated rainwater of many of its toxins.

Farmers have used riparian buffers for years to combat soil erosion from their fields. In the early 1930s, a nationwide soil conservation initiative was introduced to reduce soil erosion. In those days, a typical farm lost fifteen to twenty-five tons of soil per acre each year to erosion. With conservation programs firmly in place, the average farm now loses less than five tons per acre each year. Still, erosion washes 4.5 billion tons of sediment into America's streams and rivers each year.

Removing vegetation from a stream embankment causes erosion that will soon choke this stream with sediment.

Not only is fertile soil lost from farm fields, but the excess sediment also clogs downstream reaches causing bank erosion and flooding. By sheer volume, sediment is the number one water pollutant in our country.

Sediment in runoff from urban and suburban land is also a serious problem. Leaving a riparian buffer or establishing a no-mow zone along a stream bank filters sediments and toxins out of overland runoff and, just as importantly, helps hold the stream bank soil in place and prevent erosion.

If you must mow down to the waters edge, raise the mower blade to its highest setting and be careful not to scalp the grass off the soil. A small patch of bare soil along a stream can quickly expand into a large gully or bank undercut.

Choose the plants carefully when establishing a riparian buffer. Many non-native species sold as ground cover are touted for their ability to spread and establish quickly. The trouble is that many of these plants don't stop spreading at the stream bank and soon displace native plants. Planting native grasses, shrubs, trees, and flowers in a riparian buffer provides food and cover for native animals and helps maintain biological diversity.

Armoring a stream bank with landscape timbers or stone to prevent erosion is an expensive alternative to working with nature to achieve the same goal. Establishing deep-rooted trees and plants along a stream bank prevents erosion, cleanses storm water, and provides a beautiful green zone of protection along our waterways.

Clean water provides recreational opportunities for people and habitat for beneficial animals and plants. *Illustration by Simeon Cochran*

Horsetail

Edging and Mulching Your Garden

Chances are that your rain garden will be bordered by lawn. Where this is the case, you'll want to establish some sort of edging to keep lawn grasses from invading your garden. The two main options are to hand edge twice a year using a sharp, flat spade to cut a neat edge around your garden or to install a barrier of some type. When it comes to barriers, usually it's worth paying more for a material. Consider a high quality metal edging buried four inches or more into the soil completely surrounding areas where turf can sneak in. If you go with black plastic edging, use construction grade to avoid having to replace it in a few years.

Mulching your rain garden is a very good idea. It not only helps keeps the weeds down, it also helps maintain soil moisture, remove pollutants, and prevent erosion of the soil. You'll find that most rain gardening references recommend mulching your garden after planting. This certainly is an option. However, putting the mulch down before you plant is easier and reduces the chances you will harm your tender new plants in the process of spreading the mulch. It will also reduce the soil compaction that can result from walking around on bare soil.

Cover the entire prepared garden bed with two to three inches of an organic mulch. Shredded bark works well. It is readily available, is more refined than wood chips, and tends to stay in place better than other mulches. Lighter mulches, such as pine bark nuggets or cedar chips, will float right out of the garden during a heavy downpour. Shredded bark tends to stick together in a mat when a rain garden fills with water and usually settles back into the same spot when the water subsides.

Do not use grass clippings as mulch. Decomposing grass clippings are a source of excess nutrients that can flow into a storm drain system and be harmful to wetlands.

To determine how much mulch to buy, keep in mind that a cubic yard of mulch will cover approximately one hundred square feet when spread three inches deep. A ten by twenty foot garden (200 square feet) will require about two cubic yards of mulch.

You will want to install some type of barrier between your rain garden and any neighboring lawn grasses. © *Connie Taillon*

Shopping for plants and flowers at a greenhouse. ©Christy Thompson/Shutterstock.com

Purchasing Plants

Potted plants are the best way to go when planting a rain garden. Container plants become established quickly and give you a better-looking garden sooner. Your best success will come with plants with a well-established root system. For perennials and grasses, go with a container size of at least four inches; larger if you can afford it. Shrubs and trees should obviously be in containers proportionate to their size.

If cost is a concern, consider using plugs if you can find them. Plugs are small, cone-shaped pots, usually about two inches in diameter and about five inches long. They are often sold in six- or nine-packs like annuals. Plugs usually establish themselves rather quickly and do just as well as container plants in the long run. Shrubs and even some trees are available bare-root in spring. This is another way to reduce your costs.

Seeding is not usually recommended for rain gardens. It is too easy for the seeds to float away before they germinate. And most perennials take at least two growing seasons to become established from seed. In the meantime, weeds can move in and make it difficult for the uneducated eye to differentiate between good seedlings and bad. You can start plants from seed indoors and grow them for a few months before moving them outside. But because you are probably looking at a variety of species, the time and money spent growing all the different plants often makes it less economical.

If you are using native plants, be sure to purchase plants from a native-plant nursery that grows its own seed stock. The plants should be "nursery propagated," not just "nursery grown," which can indicate they were dug from the wild and grown in the nursery. Never dig plants from the wild unless you are part of a plant rescue group that is authorized to save a population that is slated to be destroyed.

Be sure to purchase your native plants from a reputable nursery that does not dig plants from the wild.

Careful thought
should be given before
choosing a spot for
hard-to-transplant
plants like silphiums.

Planting

Planting a rain garden really isn't any different from planting a traditional garden. The main thing is to be sure to place the plants in their proper saturation zones within in the garden.

The best time to put most plants in the ground is spring because it gives them ample time to become established before they have to endure their first winter in the ground. Container-grown summer- and fall-blooming flowers and most woody plants can be planted in spring or fall—actually all season long if you are diligent about watering when needed. You may also need to provide shelter from the sun for a few weeks. It is best to plant or transplant early blooming species right after they flower, usually in late spring. Bare-root plants shipped by mail-order nurseries should only be planted in the spring.

Plant spacing depends on each individual species and how long you want to wait for your garden to fill in, but generally about twelve inches is good for most herbaceous perennial plants. Shrubs should be planted a minimum of three feet apart. Obviously the more plants you can afford, the sooner your rain garden will be more attractive and the fewer weed problems you will have. However, planting too densely can be a waste of money and effort.

It is a good idea to place the container plants in the mulched garden before putting them in the ground to see the big picture. You may find that you didn't buy quite enough plants to cover an area, in which case you may want to space them farther apart, or you may find that you have too many of some plants and need to plant them in other areas of your garden. Some plants, such as silphiums and milkweeds, have extensive root systems and don't like to be moved once they are established. Careful thought should be given to placing these plants because they don't respond well to transplanting.

Make sure the plants are well watered in their containers right up until the time they go into the ground. Potted plants need to be carefully removed from their containers. If grown in a loose soil-less mix, shake off the excess and plant them like bare-root plants. If roots are circling, disentangle them to encourage outward growth. If the root ball is dense, use a sharp knife to cut through some of the roots. Cutting may sound harsh, but the roots must be free to move into the surrounding soil.

Try to avoid stepping in your garden as much as possible when planting. Start in the middle and work your way out. Pull away the mulch and prepare a planting hole deep enough so that the plant will go into the ground at the same level as it was growing in the nursery container. To plant bare root plants, dig the hole wider and deeper than the largest roots. Make a cone of soil in the bottom of the hole, and spread the roots out over the cone. Gently add soil as needed to keep the plant's crown at the right level, making sure to fill in the hole completely with soil to avoid air pockets where the roots may dry out. Then gently pull the mulch back up around the plant, keeping it a few inches away from the stem itself.

Give your newly planted garden a good soaking right after installation regardless of the soil moisture levels. You may also want to stick the plant tags next to the plants to help you remember what you planted and differentiate from weeds that may appear.

It's often a good idea to put labels next to your newly installed rain garden plants.

Care Right After Planting

Your new transplants will require watering their first growing season if rainfall is inadequate. Keep soil adequately moist until new plants have a full year of growth. One to two inches of water every three days for the first month is a good goal, with additional water as needed throughout the first growing season. After the first year most plants won't require additional water except in extreme dry spells.

Trees and shrubs need to be watered regularly for at least the first full year after planting. In hot weather they may need supplemental water once or twice a week. If autumn is dry, continue watering until the first hard frost. Once fully established—after three to four years—most native woody plants should be self-sufficient as far as watering.

One thing your newly planted garden won't need is fertilizer. This will only encourage weeds. And there is a very good chance a granular fertilizer will wash away before the tiny plant roots have a chance to take it up.

Until your plants have fully developed root systems, they are susceptible to washing away during strong storms. A few strategically placed deterrents, usually large rocks, will help break the flow of water and reduce your chances of washing out plants and mulch. You can also construct some sort of "dam" to prevent water from entering your garden during the first month or so after planting. However, be sure that the redirected runoff doesn't cause problems in other parts of your yard. If your water is coming from a downspout, consider disconnecting or rerouting it until your plants have a few weeks to establish. It may be frustrating to have your newly planted rain garden go unused for a while, but it will be worth it in the long run.

A carefully placed deterrent, such as a grouping of rocks, will help prevent your young plants from washing out with the full force of the water entering your garden.

MAINTAINING YOUR RAIN GARDEN

There's no getting around the fact that all gardens need some maintenance. The good news is that if you've prepared your soil correctly and chosen appropriate plants, a rain garden should not need nearly as much care and tending as a traditional garden or landscape, especially if you are using mainly native plants. The need to water and fertilize is all but eliminated once these plants are established, and the need for pesticides to kill insects or diseases is absent or rare. In fact, the use of pesticides carries a high risk of contaminating ground water, so they should be used with great caution, if at all.

Your end goals when it comes to maintenance should be to have a rain garden that is working properly, is aesthetically pleasing to you, and is easily maintained at a level that suits your time and interest. © *Connie Taillon*

One of the most important aspects of rain garden maintenance is making sure nothing interferes with the main purpose of water infiltration. Here again, proper site preparation and plant selection go a long way. But things will change as your plants grow and move around, and you will need to make regular inspections of your garden to make sure it is working properly.

If your rain garden is in the front yard or if you just want a showier garden, there are a few grooming tasks that will help the plants grow better and keep your landscape looking more tended. The amount of grooming you do will depend on the plants you are growing, where you are growing them, and how much time you like to spend tending your garden.

Rain Garden Maintenance Calendar

Early Spring
As with all gardening, spring is a busy time. But the more you do in spring, the less you will have to do the rest of the year.

Remove Winter Mulch
If you have applied winter mulch, you should remove it in early spring just as the plants begin poking above ground and when all danger of a "hard" frost is past. It's not always easy to know when this is, but if the ground starts to thaw and the soil starts to look muddy, it's usually time to start gently raking off the mulch. If you wait too long high temperatures can cause the plants to overheat and even rot.

Grasses should be cut back in early spring before they start showing any signs of new growth.

Cut Back Plants
Early spring is the best time to cut your plants back and clean out your garden. This can be done as soon as the snow melts and the soil is dry enough that you can walk in your garden without compacting it. The tools you'll use depend on the size of your garden and your plants. If you have a lot of grasses, a string trimmer or hedge shears often will work better than hand pruners. Don't cut all the way to the ground or you may damage the plant crowns. And be sure to keep the trimmer away shrubs and trees. Leave about two inches of stubble and rake off the loose debris. If possible, make several small piles of the debris along the edges of your garden so that any beneficial insects or their eggs can continue their life cycles. The debris is also a great addition to the compost pile.

Remove Weeds

Weeds will start showing up as soon as the snow cover recedes, often before your desirable plants, especially if you are growing native plants. This makes it easy to spot weeds and get rid of them while they are still small and easy to pull. A weekly weed-pulling walk through your garden in spring will do wonders. Be sure to remove the entire root system or rhizome, but be careful not to uproot neighboring plants. Use a weeding tool to get leverage if needed.

An important first step in the war with weeds is to be able to identify which plants are weeds as early in their life cycles as possible. This is challenging, especially for new gardeners who are afraid to pull seedlings because they think they may be desirable plants rather than weeds. Experience will help you to overcome this fear. Invest in a good weed identification guide and use it regularly. *Weeds of the Northern U.S. and Canada* (France Royer and Richard Dicksinson, 1999, Lone Pine Publishing) is a good choice because it includes color photographs of weeds at various stages of their life cycles, including the seedling stage.

During your weed walks, you'll want to clean out any debris, such as leaves and roofing grit, that may have ended up in your garden, especially if it has accumulated in areas where water enters your garden and can block the flow. If your garden is near a road that is sanded in winter, you may also need to clean out any sand that has accumulated.

Add Mulch

Organic mulch is continually decaying and adding organic matter to the soil. Once the garden is clean and weed-free, you may need to add additional mulch to maintain your desired two to three inches. Remember mulch helps prevent mud from splashing on plants, keeps weeds down, moderates soil temperatures, and reduces the need for supplemental watering. Mulch also keeps the soil evenly moist, which aids in water infiltration. Unmulched gardens may develop a hard soil crust that can become almost impervious to water.

Once your garden is established and filled in with desirable plants, a layer of well-rotted compost is a better alternative to shredded-bark mulch. It does all the good stuff mulch does, but also adds nutrients at a slow and steady rate and improves soil texture, helping plants grow better. And it gives you a way to recycle your yard waste into a useful product. For help on making your own compost, seed the sidebar on page 127.

Early spring is a good time to cover your rain garden with a fresh layer of compost.

Prune Shrubs

One last early spring task to consider is pruning. Many shrubs don't require a lot of pruning and shaping, and actually often look best when left to grow naturally. But some annual removal of dead or dying branches and older branches will keep your shrubs looking better and improve flowering. If your rain garden is along the street or your driveway, you may also need to prune trees and shrubs to maintain sight lines.

Summer-flowering shrubs bloom on new growth produced in the current growing season and are best pruned in early spring if you didn't prune them in winter. Don't wait too long, however, or you may cut off flower buds, which start to form right away in spring. Shrubs to prune in early spring include red-twigged dogwood, smooth hydrangea, chokeberries, and summersweet.

Low-maintenance shrub roses like 'Delicata' are beautiful additions to rain gardens.

Making Compost

Compost is created by mixing high-carbon and high-nitrogen materials proportionately with air and moisture. High-carbon materials include straw, hay, leaves, sawdust, shredded newspaper, and pine needles. High-nitrogen materials are generally succulent green plant parts like grass clippings, weeds, perennial prunings, and vegetables. If you aren't able to provide enough of the high-nitrogen materials from your garden, you may need to add animal manure, blood meal, or cottonseed meal. Kitchen scraps like eggshells, vegetables and fruits, and coffee grounds can also be added to the compost pile. Do not add meat scraps, bones, or grease, which attract rodents and other pests.

Compost ready to be added to the rain garden.

There is debate about whether or not you should add diseased plants or weeds with seed heads to the compost pile. Some experts feel the heat of a properly working compost pile will be enough to kill off the diseases and seeds. Others don't think it's worth the risk. To be on the safe side, you should probably avoid both.

Most people build or purchase some type of bin to contain their compost, but you can compost by simply piling the debris up. An ideal location for a compost bin is one hidden from view but close enough for you to easily bring stuff to it and haul the finished compost away. It is also nice to have the compost pile near a water source so that you can add water during dry spells, but it's not necessary.

Build your compost pile as materials become available, layering carbon materials alternatively with nitrogen materials. If you have an abundance of carbon materials, put some of them on the side until more nitrogen materials become available. Too many green grass clippings can mat down and prohibit the composting process. Mix them with looser materials like straw or shredded newspaper, or allow them to dry in the sun before adding them to the pile. It's also a good idea to add thin layers of topsoil or finished compost to a new pile to introduce the decay organisms that create compost. Ideally, you will have several piles going at the same time, so you will always have some finished compost available.

Once your pile is built, you'll need to do a little regular maintenance. Add water as needed to keep the pile moist but not soggy. Turn your compost regularly—once a week if possible—to get air into the pile. If you don't turn your pile, you'll still get compost, but it will take a lot longer. If you want to speed up the composting process, turn the pile more often, add more nitrogen-rich materials, and shred or chop the carbon materials before adding them to the pile so they break down quicker. You'll know your compost is ready for the garden when it is dark, crumbly, and most of the plant parts are decomposed.

Compost is a wonderful way to enrich the soil in your rain garden and a good way to put your yard "waste" to use.

Proper pruning is critical to the health of a tree. Do not make a flush cut at the trunk. Rather, make a smooth cut at the outside edge of the collar, the swollen area where the branch meets the trunk. By keeping the collar, you will encourage callus tissue to form and heal over the cut, keeping disease organisms from entering the cut surface.

Pruning Tips

TREES

Start training young trees right after planting to encourage strong, healthy mature trees that will stand up to strong winds and storms. Avoid over pruning. Young trees need plenty of leaves to manufacture the food they need for strong root and top growth.

Strong older branches develop from young branches with a forty-five-degree angle between the trunk and the tree; these are the branches you want to retain.

Remove any branches that are rubbing against each other because the bark will eventually wear away from one or both of the branches.

Remove any suckers that may be growing around the base of the tree.

Cut branches back to a larger branch or to the trunk at the outside edge of the collar. Do not leave stubs, which will only die back and provide entry points for insects and diseases.

Never prune back the leader (the main central branch) of a tree, or you'll destroy the natural shape.

Only remove lower branches if they interfere with the use of the areas under the tree.

If you made proper pruning cuts right above collar and pruned at the right time of year, you do not need to use a wound dressing. In fact, covering a wound can do more harm than good. The exception is if you need to prune a tree at the wrong time of the year and it is susceptible to attack from a major insect pest, such as oak wilt.

SHRUBS

As with trees, it's much better if you start pruning shrubs right away when they are young and continue to do minor annual pruning each year rather than let them become overgrown and end up needing major renewal pruning. Regular pruning also helps promote healthier shrubs that produce more blooms.

Remove any dead, diseased, or damaged branches. Stand back and take a look. Then decide which branches you should remove to improve the overall shape or size of the shrub. In some cases you will be cutting branches back to a certain point, and in some cases you will be removing entire branches at the base of the shrub.

Prune branches back to outward facing buds or to a point where they meet another branch. Avoid leaving stubs of branches, which usually just die back and leave dead sticks on your plant.

If your shrub is bushier than you'd like, or if you just want to encourage new growth, remove a few of the oldest branches at ground level. Stand back and take another look and decide if you need to remove a few more branches or not. Remember that once a shrub leafs out, it will appear much larger and shrubbier than when the branches are bare.

EVERGREEN CONIFERS

Most evergreen conifers grow best if allowed to maintain their natural shape, so keep pruning to a minimum. To avoid having an evergreen shrub overgrow its spot, choose a compact or dwarf cultivar in small gardens.

Many conifers only grow from their tips, so you should make all your pruning cuts in the current season's growth. An annual shaping that only removes new growth back to a bud is best. If you prune too far back behind the foliage, the branch will die.

The best time to prune most conifers is after the new growth is completed in late spring or early summer. Remove any dead, damaged, or diseased parts of evergreens at any time of year.

ABOVE RIGHT AND RIGHT: When cutting a branch back to a bud, make the cut 1/4 inch past the bud and angle the cut upward at a forty-five-degree angle to avoid damaging the bud. If the plant has opposite buds, you can make the cut straight across.

BELOW: Dogwoods are often grown for their colorful new growth. To encourage continual new stem production, these plants should be pruned hard every year.

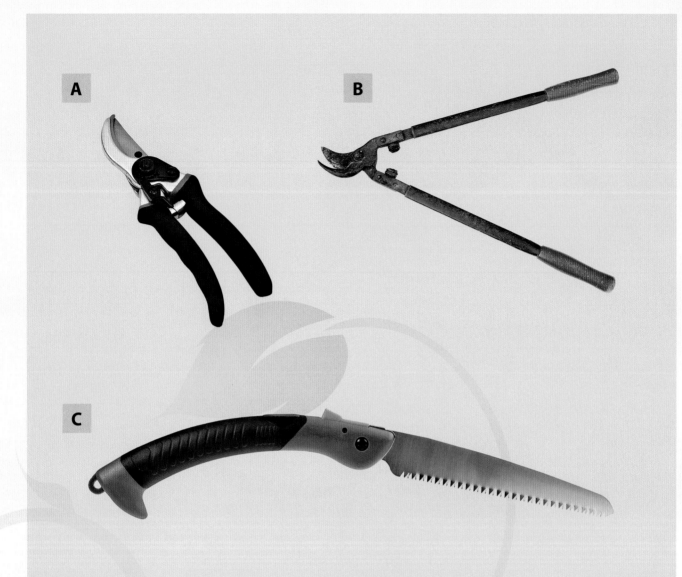

A

B

C

Gardening pruners, loppers, and a handsaw for pruning. ©Shutterstock.com: (A) Bob Mawby, (B) Edward Westmacott, (C) Simon Krzic

PRUNING TOOLS

The three tools that will get you through most pruning jobs are hand-held pruners (A), loppers (B), and a small curved saw (C). Pruning shears are available in two basic designs: bypass and anvil. Bypass shears tend to damage stems less than anvil types and can reach into tighter spots. Anvil shears are more powerful. Loppers are essentially heavy-duty bypass or anvil shears with long handles. They can cut branches up to two inches thick. A small pruning saw can be used for branches larger than that. Pruning tools are easiest to use and make the healthiest cuts when they are sharp and clean.

Place an identifying stake near newly added plants so you can find them in summer and give them the supplemental water they may need.

Mid- to Late Spring

Add Plants

Mid- to late spring is a good time to add new plants if you need to. By this time most of your plants should be up and growing and you will be able to see if you lost any to winter damage or rodent feeding. Or you may want to add a few new plants that you didn't have a chance to put in when you first planted your garden. Plants added now will have a chance to establish their root systems and get off to a strong start before they have to begin retaining water. Remember all newly installed plants require about one inch of water a week during their first growing season. Use a stake to mark newly planted seedlings so you can find them later in the summer to provide the supplemental water they may need without overwatering the entire garden.

Avoid Fertilizing

In traditional gardens, spring is the time to fertilize. Possibly one of the best arguments for using native plants is their ability to grow in soils lower in fertility than most exotic landscape plants require. Soil that is too fertile is usually more of a problem because fertile soils favor the establishment of weedy species and can also cause prairie species to grow too lush and lank.

Unless a soil test indicates that your soil is significantly lacking in one or more of the necessary nutrients, you shouldn't add synthetic fertilizers to your rain garden. There is a good chance they may just wash away down the storm sewer and make their way into nearby wetlands. Incorporating organic matter into the soil before planting and on an annual basis in established gardens should be all your plants need in the way of added nutrients.

Watering

If conditions are dry, you may need to do some supplemental watering by late spring. Keep in mind that plants do best with about one inch of water per week. Newly installed plants will need more because their roots are shallow. Remember that your goal is to water the soil, not the plants. Moisten the soil thoroughly and then allow the garden bed to dry moderately before watering again. Soaker hoses and other watering devices that evenly distribute water over the soil instead of wetting plant foliage are the best.

One of the main attractions of using native plants is to reduce or even eliminate the need for supplemental watering. If you've chosen plants correctly for your conditions, established plants will rarely need supplemental watering. In fact, because most prairie plants are adapted to soil on the drier side, too much water often leads to problems, such as root rot and the rampant growth of moisture-loving weeds.

Any trees or shrubs in your garden need to be watered regularly for at least the first full year after planting. Once fully established, after three to four years, most woody plants should not need supplemental watering.

A soaker hose.
© Michael Major/
Shutterstock.com

Controlling Tall Plants

Some taller plants may need staking, especially if your garden is located in an open, windy area. Many support systems using hoops and sticks of wood or metal are available from nurseries and home-improvement stores. Use small tomato cages for bushy plants. Long-stemmed plants will need a stake for each blooming stem. Put stakes in the ground in late spring before the plants are too tall. This helps avoid root damage and makes it easier to put the support system in place. Once plants become tall and floppy, it is very difficult to get them back up. Loosely tie plants to the stake with inconspicuous green or brown twine. It may look unsightly for a few days, but in a week or so plant foliage will cover the string and stakes.

If you don't want the maintenance of staking consider using lower-growing bushier plants or selecting dwarf or compact cultivars of taller growing species. A prime example is New England aster. The species itself can grow to six feet tall and plants often topple over in garden settings before they've even had a chance to bloom. To enjoy the late summer color and insect attracting traits offered by New England aster, select one of the many dwarf cultivars, such as 'Alma Potschke,' 'Red Star,' or 'Purple Dome.'

Cutting back taller summer and fall-flowering species in spring reduces plant height and encourages more compact growth, making these plants more suitable for landscape use. It will also reduce or eliminate the need for staking. Cutting back can also be used to stagger bloom times, extending the period of bloom for certain species. Cutting back of plants by one-half to two-thirds must be done early enough in the growing season so as not to delay flowering too long. This timing will vary in different areas of the country; in the Midwest, for example, it is best not to do any cutting or pinching back after early June. Where the growing season is longer, you could cut back plants up to about mid-June.

TOP: Any necessary staking should be done early in the growing season when plants are small and less prone to damage from the process.

CENTER: 'Purple Dome' is a compact selection of New England aster (*Symphyotrichum novae-angliae*) that doesn't require staking.

BOTTOM: Part of this planting of oxeye (*Heliopsis helianthoides*) was cut back in midspring to produce a more compact plant and extend the bloom period.

Purple coneflower seed heads in winter

Tickseed

Perennials that Can Be Cut Back in Spring to Reduce Height

Boltonia asteroides (doll's daisy, false aster)
Echinacea purpurea (purple coneflower)
Eupatoriadelphus species (Joe pye weeds)
Helenium autumnale (autumn sneezeweed)
Heliopsis helianthoides (oxeye)
Hibiscus moscheutos (rose mallow)
Lobelia cardinalis (cardinal flower)
Monarda didyma (bee balm)
Phlox maculata (meadow phlox)
Physostegia virginiana (obedient plant)
Rudbeckia species (black-eyed Susans)
Symphyotrichum novae-angliae (New England aster)
Tradescantia species (spiderworts)
Vernonia species (ironweeds)
Veronicastrum virginicum (Culver's root)

Spiderwort (*Tradescantia* species) is a plant that benefits from being divided every few years.

Showy forsythia (*Forsythia x intermedia*) is an example of a spring-blooming shrub that should be pruned right after flowering.

Dividing

Most perennial plants will benefit from being divided every three or four years. Dividing prevents overcrowding and keeps the plants healthy, vigorous, and more prone to flower production. The best time to divide most plants is spring so that they have a full growing season to recover. To divide herbaceous plants, unearth the plant with a spade or trowel, remove excess soil from roots, pull or cut apart rooted sections, and replant as soon as possible.

Some plants with deep tap roots do not respond well to attempts to divide or replant them. These include butterfly milkweed, silphiums, and blue wild indigo. Be sure to think carefully before using these plants, especially in a small rain garden.

Pruning

If you have any evergreen conifers in your rain garden that need pruning, this should be done in late spring and early summer just after you see new growth. Arborvitaes and junipers usually look best when their natural shape is maintained. It is easier to do this if you do a little pruning each spring rather than let them get too big and then try to prune them back severely.

Spring-blooming shrubs and small trees flower on buds formed the previous summer or fall. These include amelanchiers, dogwoods, forsythias, lilacs, rhododendrons, magnolias, mock oranges, spireas, and viburnums. They should be pruned as soon as possible after flowering. If you prune them in winter or spring, you will be cutting off their flower buds; this won't kill them, it will just mean you won't have flowers for one season.

Gray-headed coneflower (*Ratibida pinnata*), wild bergamot (*Monarda fistulosa*), and anise hyssop (*Agastache foeniculum*) are all beautiful but prolific seed producers; consider cutting flowers off before they have a chance to go to seed.

Summer

Weeding

Summer is a good time to do one more thorough weeding of your rain garden. The weeds that like warmer temperatures to germinate will be up and growing, but you should still get most of the cool-season weeds out before they go to seed. In established gardens, this summer weeding may be the only weeding you'll need to do until next spring.

Watering

In hot weather, plants may need supplemental water once or twice a week. Keep in mind the one inch of water per week rule.

Deadheading

Deadheading is removing spent flower buds to help stimulate prolonged and repeated blooming. It is a completely optional maintenance task that you can choose to avoid if you want to reduce your time taking care of the garden. Cut back to the next set of leaves to encourage new buds to open.

Deadheading also reduces unwanted seed production on plants that tend to set a lot of seed and can become weedy. Obviously cutting off spent flower heads eliminates seeds that provide food for wildlife. However, if you allowed every flower to set seed you would be overwhelmed with seedlings in just one growing season.

Fall

Watering

If the autumn season is dry, continue watering until the first hard frost, especially any newly planted items.

Cutting Plants Back

Although it's not something usually advocated because of their usefulness as sources of food and shelter for wildlife, you may want to cut back at least some of your taller plants in fall. This won't harm the plants. One of the biggest objections city officials and neighbors will have about using native plants is that they look "dead" and "weedy" in winter. So if it gets you through the process without too many issues, it may be worth cutting back your taller plants in fall, especially if your rain garden is in the front yard.

Whether or not you decide to cut back your plants at this time of year is really a matter of aesthetics. It doesn't affect how the plants grow. With many nonnative plants, this cutting back is recommended to reduce the chance of diseases and insects overwintering. This isn't as much of a factor with native plants because they aren't really plagued by pest problems that overwinter in plant parts. Some gardeners like to cut back some of the rougher looking plants in fall and allow the showier plants to remain until spring. This also has the advantage of spreading out the maintenance.

It's up to you whether you want to leave your plants standing over winter or cut them back in fall.

Winter

Winter Mulch

In colder climates, you may want to apply winter mulch if you are growing plants that aren't reliably hardy in your area or if you planted anything in fall. Winter mulch offers added protection from the freezing and thawing that can result in frost heaving of plants. Winter mulch should be laid down after the ground has frozen to keep the cold in and keep your plants dormant. If you put it down too early, it acts as an insulator and the ground can remain warm too long.

The best mulch is a reliable snow cover. However, you can't count on that, cover marginally hardy or newly planted or divided perennials with three to four inches of a loose material, such as straw, pine needles, or shredded leaves, after temperatures have dropped to below 25 degrees Fahrenheit.

Dormant Pruning

Almost every tree and shrub in your landscape will need pruning at one time or another, and the better job you do, the healthier your plants will be. Proper pruning not only encourages healthier plants, it also helps plants look neater and tidier in the landscape.

The keys to successful pruning are appropriate timing and the right tools. Most trees and shrubs are best pruned in their dormant period, reducing the chance of infection from insects and diseases. You can also see a deciduous plant's silhouette when the leaves are off.

Pruning tools must be sharp and clean. The basic pruning tool is a hand-held bypass pruner. Larger shrubs and small trees will require loppers and a pruning saw. If you have large trees in need of major pruning, you should have it done by a professional tree trimmer.

Pruning is somewhat subjective, but there are some basic rules to follow. Always remove dead wood and branches that rub against each other. It is usually best to try to maintain the natural shape of a tree or shrub. In general, do not remove more than one-third of the branches in one pruning. However, overgrown deciduous shrubs may need renewal pruning; cut them all the way back to the ground in early spring.

Winter is the best time to prune suckers and other errant branches from woody species.

Maintain a cover of decorative rock to protect the ground where concentrated water flows into the rain garden from a pipe or swale. © *Connie Taillon*

Long-Term Maintenance

A rain garden should not only be maintained to look good and be healthy, but also to be functional in its role to retain rainwater. It should be obvious to you when things are not working right. But you should do some periodic checks to make sure they are.

Examine the berm, inflow, and overflow for signs of erosion. If you notice rills and gullies caused by erosion, bring more soil in to fill them and then replant as soon as possible. If erosion is a persistent problem, there may be too much water flowing in too rapidly. If this is the case, you may need to reduce the slope of the pipe or swale directing water to the garden or somehow cut back on the amount of water entering your garden. A cover of decorative rock in areas where water flow is concentrated will help slow the rate of flow.

You should never see water in your garden three days after a one-inch storm. If water is retained for longer than seventy-two hours, your soil air spaces may be clogged with fine sediment, which could be washed in with rainwater or come from disintegration of mulch. If sediment is coming in with water, try to find out the source and stabilize the area. If your mulch is the cause, remove the mulch, rough up the soil surface, and redistribute the loosened mulch.

Lingering water could also indicate that you did not properly prepare your soil before planting. In this case you'll need to amend your soil with compost and sand as described in Chapter 1.

As plants grow and develop deeper root systems, this will improve the soil's ability to soak up rainwater. After a few years, retest the infiltration rate in your garden. If it has increased significantly, you may need to raise the garden wall or outlet so the garden can hold back more water.

Leaf spot diseases often show up on black-eyed Susan (*Rudbeckia* 'Goldsturm').

Monarda species are often afflicted with powdery mildew.

Possible Pest Problems

The key in pest management is to really get to know your garden and the plants in it. If you spot a problem, identify it correctly (get help from a local expert, if needed), find out what is causing it, and decide if it is serious enough to warrant attention. Most pest problems are purely cosmetic and won't do any long-term damage to your plants. You have to decide what your level of tolerance is and determine whether you want to take action or live with the problem. There is an increased risk of ground water contamination from pesticides in rain gardens with rapid water movement, so avoid their use whenever possible.

Keep in mind that many problems are due to cultural or planting conditions rather than insects or diseases. Yellowing or browning foliage, stunted growth, and buds that rot before opening could be signs that you have poor soil drainage or your plants are overcrowded. Once again, making sure you have the right plant for the site and the appropriate soil conditions is the best way to avoid such problems.

Diseases and Viruses

Diseases are rare on most of the recommended rain garden plants. If they do occur, they are rarely serious and can usually be prevented the next year by altering cultural practices, such as changing watering habits or thinning out some plants. Prevention in the form of good site selection and proper planting distance is the best way to avoid disease problems. If disease problems become severe, you'll need to pull up the infected plants and choose another plant for that spot.

Aster yellows can be a problem on several prairie plants, including *Gaillardia*, *Echinacea* and *Aster* species. It is caused by a virus-like organism spread by leafhopper feeding. Plants become discolored and have irregular, stunted growth and often flowers do not open. There is no cure for plants infected with aster yellows. It is usually best to dig up infected plants and find something else better suited to the location.

Rudbeckia species (especially the popular cultivar 'Goldsturm') can be afflicted with several leaf spot diseases, especially when they are grown in landscapes and gardens where overhead watering is used and the disease organisms are easily splashed from plant to plant. While these diseases rarely kill plants, they can make the foliage quite unsightly. Here again, there is probably a better plant choice for these garden situations.

Powdery mildew is often seen on rain garden plants. To reduce chances of infection, increase air circulation by pruning out inside branches and removing some nearby plants. If you want to make the effort to control this disease on landscape plantings, Cornell University has developed a baking-soda-based spray: Mix 1 tablespoon baking soda and 1 tablespoon horticultural oil with 1 gallon of water. Spray each plant completely about once a week, starting before infections appear. It's a good idea to test the spray on a few leaves before spraying the entire plant to make sure the spray won't do more damage than the disease.

Here are a few key things to remember in deterring diseases: Many fungal diseases require water on plant leaves to develop. Avoid wetting leaves when watering by using methods that water the soil, not the plants. Diseases often develop on plants that are stressed, so keep your plants as healthy as possible. Once a disease has infected a plant, prune off diseased tissue as soon as possible and destroy it to get rid of the pathogen.

Insects

The first thing to keep in mind when talking about insects in a garden is that most are not only harmless but are vital to the health of a garden or landscape. Douglas Tallamy points out in *Bringing Nature Home*, "Of the 9 million or so insect species on earth, a mere 1 percent interact with humans in negative ways. The other 99 percent of the insect species pollinate plants, return nutrients tied up in dead plants and animals to the soil, keep populations of insect herbivores in check, aerate and enrich the soil, and . . . provide food either directly or indirectly for most other animals." He also makes the case that these beneficial insects can only survive in a landscape or garden "if there are enough different types of prey available for them at all stages of their life cycle."

In fact, some insect damage is a good thing. It shows that your garden is a biodiverse habitat providing important food sources for the native insects that are the basis of our entire food chain. Consequently, the first thing you need to do with insects is accurately identify them as friend or foe. Some of the well-known "good guys" are predators like lady beetles, walking sticks, wasps, and praying mantis. But the list of insects that should also be considered beneficial based on their importance as bird food includes unlikely candidates like grasshoppers and locusts, plant bugs, lace bugs, leafhoppers, and spiders. Dragonflies are important mosquito eaters, and remember that those hungry caterpillars turn into beautiful butterflies and moths.

Aphids and leaf miners may show up in your rain garden. In most cases neither will be life-threatening to your plants and can be tolerated in larger gardens, but in landscape situations, these insects will make your plants unsightly. Aphids tend to be bigger problems during hot, dry spells. They especially like oxeye, asters, black-eyed Susans, and phloxes. If you see aphids appearing on your plants, give them daily blasts of water with your garden hose to dislodge the insects before they can become too numerous.

TOP: Bees are among the many beneficial insects you will find in your rain garden.

BOTTOM: Leafminer damage is usually only cosmetic and doesn't require any action other than removing infected leaves.

Four-lined plant bug damage is unsightly but not usually life-threatening.

Keep in mind that most plants can tolerate quite a bit of insect feeding before they are actually harmed by it. Even if you do have a large population of Japanese beetles or another devastating feeder, it's still never worth it to use insecticides. Not only are they toxic to you and your garden guests, they destroy too many beneficial insects. If an insect problem becomes so bad that the health of your plant is questionable, you should consider replacing the plant with something better suited to the conditions. It's cruel to lure wildlife to your landscape and then use herbicides, insecticides, and other pesticides that can poison and destroy them.

Many people worry about rain gardens attracting mosquitoes. In truth, a properly working rain garden is more of a way to rid your yard of this pest. Mosquitoes lay eggs in standing water and the larva hatch into the flying insect three to seven days later. So if your rain garden drains properly, within twenty-four hours, the eggs will actually dry up and die before they hatch, thus killing the mosquitoes.

Other Animal Pests

Deer and rabbits are usually more serious problems than any insects that may visit your rain garden. They are also much more difficult to control. There are many repellents available. All of them are temporary solutions, however, and they require a lot of time and effort to be effective, especially against deer.

Owning a large dog can be effective in deterring deer. But the best long-term solution for a serious deer problem is to install some type of fencing, which must be at least eight feet tall to be effective and often isn't very attractive. Rabbit fences should be three feet deep and made of a wire mesh too dense for them to squeeze through.

You can also make plant choices based on deer feeding. Although no plant can really be considered "deer proof" under all conditions, deer generally avoid plants with thorns, aromatic plants, and plants with leathery, fuzzy, or hairy foliage.

Joe pye weed

Sneezeweed

Goldenrod

New England aster

Rain Garden Plants Rarely or Seldom Damaged by Deer

No plant can be counted on to be entirely resistant to deer feeding, but these plants tend to be the least favorites of deer and other herbivores.

Perennials

Achillea 'Moonshine' (moonshine yarrow)
Actaea racemosa (bugbane)
Allium cernuum (nodding wild onion)
Amsonia species (blue stars)
Aquilegia species (columbines)
Asarum canadense (wild ginger)
Asclepias species (milkweeds)
Baptisia australis (blue wild indigo)
Boltonia asteroides (doll's daisy)
Chelone species (turtleheads)
Coreopsis verticillata (threadleaf coreopsis)
Echinacea purpurea (purple coneflower)
Eupatoriadelphus maculatus (Joe pye weed)
Geranium maculatum (wild geranium)
Helenium species (sneezeweeds)
Iris species (iris, blue flags)
Lobelia species (cardinal flower, lobelia)
Matteuccia struthiopteris (ostrich fern)
Monarda species (bee balm, wild bergamot)
Physostegia virginiana (obedient plant)
Rudbeckia species (black-eyed Susans)
Solidago species (goldenrods)
Symphyotrichum species (asters)
Tiarella cordifolia (foamflower)
Veronicastrum virginicum (Culver's root)

Grasses

Andropogon gerardii (big bluestem)
Carex pensylvanica (Pennsylvania sedge)
Chasmanthium latifolium (northern sea oats)
Helictotrichon sempervirens (blue oat grass)
Panicum virgatum (switchgrass)
Schizachyrium scoparium (little bluestem)
Sorghastrum nutans (Indiangrass)

Shrubs and Trees

Acer species (maples)
Amelanchier species (serviceberries)
Betula nigra (river birch)
Clethra alnifolia (summersweet)
Cornus sericea (red-osier dogwood)
Hamamelis species (witch hazels)
Ilex species (winterberry, hollies)
Lindera benzoin (spicebush)
Myrica species (bayberries)
Nyssa sylvatica (black gum)
Quercus species (oaks)
Taxodium distichum (bald cypress)
Viburnum species (viburnums)

PLANT INDEX

The list of plants suitable for rain gardens is quite extensive. A plant's suitability is based on where you live (hardiness and native species), where your rain garden is located on your property (sun or shade, front or back yard), and how you want your rain garden to look (plant height, year-round interest, flower color). The plants featured in the Plant Index were selected because of their high suitability for rain gardens and their availability in the nursery trade. Some may not be available at traditional nurseries and garden centers but are available at nurseries specializing in native plants. At the end of each section, you'll find additional suggestions for plants that can be considered.

Spiderwort (*Tradescantia*), prairie phlox (*Phlox pilosa*), black-eyed Susan (*Rudbeckia*), and stiff tickseed (*Coreopsis palmate*) combine to create a stunning midsummer show.

The fiddlehead of an ostrich fern (*Matteuccia struthiopteris*) is often a first sign of spring in the rain garden.

Plants are generally grouped into perennials, which includes groundcovers and ferns; grasses; shrubs and small trees; and trees and then listed alphabetically by genus. The most recognized common names are included.

Hardiness information is based on the USDA Plant Hardiness Zone Map found on page 186. Hardiness zones indicate the severity of winter temperatures. The lower the number, the more severe the winter climate. While it is important to know your hardiness zone, don't live and die by it. Use it as a guideline. A plant's ability to survive winter is affected by many factors, such as snow cover, soil moisture, the plant's age, and winter mulching.

Native or Nonnative indicates the plant's indigenous status. Native plants are those that grew in North America before the natural landscape was substantially affected by European settlement. If you want to find out which plants were native in your area, you should consult a reference specific to your state or area, such as your state Department of Natural Resources's plant heritage website.

Mature height is the typical height of the plant in flower after it is fully established in a garden or landscape. Remember that many factors can affect plant height, including available sunlight, soil moisture, and fertility levels. And also keep in mind that plants in the middle of the rain garden will often appear up to a foot shorter because they are planted in a lower area of the garden.

Planting zones are the recommended areas within the rain garden where the plant will do best. They are based mainly on the plant's tolerance for water saturation, but consideration is also given to the plant's mature height. Zone A plants tolerate periodic or frequent standing or flowing water but also withstand seasonal dry spells. They are often taller plants, and thus better suited for the bottom of the rain garden. Zone B plants tolerate periodically moist or saturated soil during larger storms. They will do better planted along the sides of the garden where there is average to dry soil moisture, outside of Zone A but inside Zone C. Zone C plants are generally shorter plants that tolerate drier conditions but can also withstand the infrequent saturation of soil that can occur. This zone is usually the most visible and it is the area where the rain garden will blend into the existing landscape.

Sunlight requirements are indicated by the icons and range from full sun to partial sun to shade. Full sun means at least six hours of direct sun daily. Partial sun is roughly three to six hours of direct sun a day. Shade is anything less than three hours of sun a day.

In the description paragraph, you'll find information about the plant's growth habits, flowering and foliage characteristics, and seasonal interest as well as maintenance when it differs from the general information in Chapter 4. You'll also find information about required soil conditions, such as pH levels, if they vary greatly from what is typically found in rain gardens and described in Chapter 1.

Cultivars are selections readily available in the nursery trade that offer characteristics different enough from the species that warrant their consideration for rain garden use. Whenever possible, consider using species and natural varieties indigenous to your area to ensure genetic diversity and provide optimum habitat for native fauna.

Other species are members of the genus that are also well-adapted to rain garden use. Some are native to other areas of the country and are as suitable for rain garden use as the main plant for their native areas; it was just a coin toss to decide which species got top billing.

Perennials

'Moonshine' yarrow

Bugbane

Maidenhair fern

Achillea 'Moonshine'
Moonshine yarrow
> USDA Zones 3 to 8
>
> Nonnative
>
> 1 to 2 feet tall
>
> Zones B, C

Species of *Achillea* are quite aggressive, but this compact cultivar does well in garden settings. It has fernlike, gray-green leaves and lemon yellow flowers throughout most of the summer. Deadheading promotes additional bloom. Spent flower stems can be cut back after flowering to improve appearance. Plants may need staking on windy sites; heavy rains can also flatten plants. Tolerates alkaline soils.

Actaea racemosa (Cimicifuga racemosa)
Bugbane, black cohosh, black baneberry, black snakeroot
> USDA Zones 3 to 8
>
> Native
>
> 4 to 6 feet tall
>
> Zone A

This upright, stately plant has abundant creamy white flowers in summer. The spikes of fluffy flowers rise well above the mounded foliage on wiry stems and are sources of pollen for many insects. The deeply cut foliage is an attractive deep green color and offers landscape interest when plants aren't in flower. The tall stems may droop under the weight of their flowers or flop over in strong winds. These plants like a little morning sun; when grown in heavy shade, flowers stalks bend toward the light. Leaves may scorch during dry periods. Plants are slow to establish but long-lived. They eventually become quite large and can crowd out nearby plants. Deadhead to prevent unwanted seedlings.

Adiantum pedatum
Maidenhair fern
> USDA Zones 2 to 8
>
> Native
>
> 1 to 2 feet tall
>
> Zone B

Maidenhair fern has horizontal, lacy, fan-shaped, arching branches and wiry, black stems. This delicate fern is attractive from spring through fall, and its fine texture brings softness to a shaded rain garden. Transplant it carefully to avoid damaging the thin stems. It requires adequate water during establishment but is quite drought tolerant once established; fronds may turn brown in late summer though. With time, 2-foot-wide clumps will cover the ground. Prefers slightly acidic soil, but tolerates alkaline soils.

Nodding wild onion

'Blue Ice' eastern bluestar

Canadian anemone

Allium cernuum
Nodding wild onion
> USDA Zones 3 to 8
> Native
> 12 to 18 inches tall
> Zone C

Nodding onion has grasslike, flattened leaves about 12 inches long in neat clumps that resemble chives. The nodding flowers are held nicely above the foliage on slightly bent stems. They can be white to pink to lavender and bloom for about a month starting midsummer. The foliage is attractive into late summer and the papery dried seed heads are decorative in autumn. Plants will naturalize by self-seeding and expand outward by bulb offsets in optimum growing conditions but rarely become pesky. Deadhead flowers before seeds set to control unwanted seedlings. Tolerates a slightly higher pH.

Amsonia tabernaemontana
Eastern bluestar, willow amsonia
> USDA Zones 3 to 9
> Native
> 2 to 3 feet tall
> Zone B

Bluestars are erect, clumping plants with clusters of light blue, starlike flowers in late spring. The narrow, willow-shaped foliage may turn an attractive golden yellow in fall. Plants may require staking, especially if they are in shade. Plants can be cut back by one-half to one-third after flowering for a neater appearance.

Cultivars: 'Blue Ice' is a compact selection that only grows 15 to 18 inches tall and has darker blue flowers and more reliable fall color.

Other species: *A. ciliata* (fringed bluestar) has narrower leaves and will do better in southern rain gardens. USDA zones 5 to 9.

A. hubrichtii (Hubricht's bluestar) has narrower leaves, giving it an almost feathery texture. USDA zones 5 to 9.

A. illustris (Ozark bluestar) has shinier, thicker leaves. USDA zones 4 to 9.

Anemone canadensis
Canadian anemone, windflower
> USDA Zones 2 to 8
> Native
> 12 to 18 inches tall
> Zones A, B

Canadian anemone has long-stalked, snowy white, 2-inch flowers held well above the foliage. They first appear in mid- to late spring and bloom well into early summer. A large planting is quite striking when in bloom. The attractive leaves are deeply divided into three to seven lobes with toothed margins. This plant is quite aggressive and rhizomes are difficult to eradicate once established, so it is best used in large rain gardens. Plants tolerate a wide range of soil types and sunlight levels, and are less aggressive in drier soil and in shade than they are in moist soil in full sun. Plants may go dormant during extremely dry conditions.

Other species: *A. hupehensis* var. *japonica* (Japanese anemone) and *A.* x *hybrida* (hybrid anemone, Japanese anemone) are groups of nonnative hybrids that bloom late summer into fall and have white or pink flowers. Popular selections are 'September Charm' and 'Honorine Jobert.' Plants are not nearly as aggressive as Canada anemone, but they will spread. They grow anywhere from 1½ to 4 feet tall and are best suited for use in rain garden Zone B in full sun to partial shade. USDA zones 4 to 8.

Canada columbine

Aquilegia canadensis
Canada columbine
> USDA Zones 3 to 9
> Native
> 12 to 24 inches tall
> Zones B, C

This graceful, erect plant has nodding, upside-down, red and yellow flowers with five, upward-spurred petals dangling from the tips of branching stems. The grayish leaves are compound, divided into lobed leaflets grouped in threes. The plant blooms from mid spring to early summer. It will self-seed, but not to the point of becoming a pest. Old rootstocks do not transplant well. Leafminers may attack the foliage, causing tan tunnels or blotches. Remove and destroy affected leaves as soon as you see them.

Cultivars: 'Corbett' is a pale yellow selection. 'Little Lanterns' is a diminutive selection growing only 8 to 10 inches tall.

Other species: *A. formosa* (western columbine) is a similar-looking western species. USDA zones 4 to 8.

Goat's beard

Aruncus dioicus
Goat's beard
> USDA Zones 3 to 8
> Native
> 3 to 5 feet tall
> Zone B

This robust plant has attractive foliage and flowers. The white plumes of feathery flowers appear in late spring and are held nicely above the cut leaf foliage. The flowers attract many pollinating insects. Plants are dioecious—male and female flowers on separate plants—but there really isn't any major difference between the flowers' appearance. Plants will self sow and may be cut back after flowering to reduce seedlings. No pest problems, but leaves may scorch if plants receive too much sun. Plants form large colonies with time that are difficult to divide.

Wild ginger

Butterfly milkweed

Lady fern

Asarum canadense

Wild ginger

> USDA Zones 3 to 8
>
> Native
>
> 6 to 8 inches tall
>
> Zone C

Wild ginger is a rhizomatous creeping plant with large, textured, heart-shaped leaves up to 8 inches wide. The leaves are up early in spring, and they cover the interesting nodding, maroon flowers that appear in midspring. This plant provides excellent groundcover for the edges of rain gardens in shady areas. Plants may wilt during dry spells but will quickly recover with watering. The plant spreads quickly but is easy to pull and rarely becomes invasive.

Other species: *A. caudatum* (western wild ginger) is slightly smaller and has shinier, evergreen leaves. USDA zones 5 to 8.

Asclepias tuberosa

Butterfly milkweed

> USDA Zones 3 to 8
>
> Native
>
> 1 to 3 feet tall
>
> Zones B, C

Butterfly milkweed has dense clumps of leafy stems topped with broad, flat clusters of fiery orange, red, or sometimes yellow flowers in summer. Plants may send up additional stems from the crown as they get older, giving mature plants an almost shrublike appearance. Set out young container-grown plants in their permanent locations because the deep taproots make plants difficult to move. Plants are slow to emerge in spring, so cultivate carefully until new growth appears; you may want to mark the site each fall. Plants can get a little top-heavy and may require gentle staking. Apply winter mulch in cold areas to prevent frost heaving until young plants are established. Plants rarely need dividing and they are not prolific seed producers.

Other species: *A. incarnata* (swamp milkweed) has flat, terminal clusters of pale rose to rose-purple, somewhat fragrant flowers on 2- to 4-foot, sturdy plants in summer. It grows best on constantly wet soils in full sun. It does self-seed prolifically. 'Ice Ballet' has white flowers and 'Cinderella' and 'Soulmate' have rose-pink flowers. These cultivars usually do not produce as many seedlings as the species. USDA zones 3 to 9. Rain garden zone A.

Athyrium filix-femina

Lady fern

> USDA Zones 2 to 9
>
> Native
>
> 2 to 3 feet tall
>
> Zone A, B

Lady fern forms a cool green carpet of lacy, deeply cut fronds that arch from the crown. The bright green to light yellow, triangular fronds are produced continually during growing season, keeping plants fresh-looking. The plant prefers a slightly acidic soil but tolerates higher soil pH. The fronds are somewhat brittle, and older fronds may become tattered if they are grown in windy sites or are battered by rain off a nearby roof. The plant will spread slowly from rhizomes.

Cultivars: 'Lady in Red' is a popular selection that has attractive deep red stems.

Blue wild indigo

Baptisia australis
Blue wild indigo
> USDA Zones 4 to 8
>
> Native
>
> 3 to 4 feet
>
> Zone B

Blue wild indigo has attractive bluish green compound leaves on nicely shaped, almost shrub-like, plants. The deep blue, pealike flowers occur on spikes up to 1 foot long in late spring and are very showy. They turn into ornamental charcoal gray seedpods that persist into winter. This long-lived perennial starts out slowly but eventually forms huge clumps that are difficult to transplant, so choose a site carefully. Plants rarely need dividing and resent disturbance. Trimming or shearing foliage to shape after bloom helps maintain the rounded plant appearance, but eliminates the attractive seedpods. Peony hoops placed over plants in early spring will support larger plants or those grown in shadier spots. Prefers slightly acidic soil.

Other species: *B. australis* var. *minor* is smaller than the true species, staying under 3 feet tall, and has larger flowers. USDA zones 4 to 8.

B. alba var. *macrophylla* (*B. lactaea*, *B. leucantha*; largeleaf wild indigo) grows 3 to 4 feet tall and has white flowers mid- to late spring. USDA zones 4 to 8.

B. sphaerocarpa (yellow wild indigo) only grows 2 to 3 feet tall has yellow flowers. USDA zones 5 to 9.

Doll's daisy

Boltonia asteroides
Doll's daisy
> USDA Zones 4 to 9
>
> Native
>
> 3 to 5 feet tall
>
> Zone A

Doll's daisy is an erect plant with narrow, gray-green leaves. It has small heads of white, aster-like flowers with yellow centers. It starts blooming in late summer and continues well into fall. The plant is a good source of pollen in fall when not much is still blooming. Plants may need support to keep them from flopping over. Cut them back to one-half to two-thirds in spring to encourage compact growth. Plants will spread by seed.

Cultivars: 'Nana' is a more compact selection. 'Snowbank' is a widely available selection that stays in the 3-foot range and has sturdy stems smothered in white flowers. 'Pink Beauty' has pink flowers but grows quite tall and floppy.

Pink turtlehead

Chelone lyonii
Pink turtlehead

>USDA Zones 4 to 9
>
>Native
>
>30 to 36 inches tall
>
>Zones A, B

Pink turtlehead has terminal clusters of pink, inflated, arching, two-lipped flowers that appear in late summer, bloom for about six weeks, and are followed by attractive dried seed heads. Plants have an upright to slightly vase-shaped form and narrow, dark green leaves. The root system consists of a taproot and rhizomes, which can form large colonies. Plants may need support, especially if grown in partial shade.

Other species: *C. glabra* (white turtlehead) only grows about 2 feet tall and is a bit more aggressive than pink turtlehead. It has white, sometimes pinkish, flowers. USDA zones 3 to 7.

C. obliqua (red turtlehead) is similar to pink turtlehead but native farther north and west. USDA zones 5 to 8.

'Zagreb' threadleaf tickseed

Coreopsis verticillata
Threadleaf tickseed

>USDA Zones 4 to 9
>
>Native
>
>24 to 30 inches tall
>
>Zones B, C

Threadleaf coreopsis has bright yellow flowers in summer and attractive fine-textured leaves throughout the growing season. It spreads by rhizomes to form dense clumps that are difficult to weed out. It is low maintenance in the garden and attracts a wide range of insects, including bees and butterflies.

Cultivars: 'Moonbeam,' with pale yellow flowers, and 'Zagreb,' with bright yellow flowers, are two popular selections that are easier to keep in check in gardens.

Other species: *C. lanceolata* (lanceleaf tickseed) grows about 2 feet tall and has golden yellow flowers. It is an aggressive seeder, so use with caution. Several cultivars of lanceleaf tickseed may be better choices for garden use. 'Double Sunburst' is a semi-double form. 'Goldfink' is a dwarf form with yellow ray flowers and an orange center. USDA zones 3 to 8.

C. palmata (stiff tickseed) grows 2 to 3 feet tall and flowers earlier than other *Coreopsis* species. The 1 ½- to 2-inch composite flowers are pale to bright yellow. The foliage often has reddish tints in fall and usually remains in good condition until a hard frost. Plants spread by rhizomes and can form large colonies. USDA zones 3 to 8.

C. tripteris (tall tickseed) grows 3 to 6 feet tall and likes more soil moisture, making it a good choice for rain garden Zone A. It also blooms latest, midsummer through early fall. The slightly smaller flowers have yellow petals surrounding a brown disk and appear singly on the upper stems. Plants often form loose colonies and are prolific seeders, so tall tickseed is best used in large rain gardens, where it provides a soft cloud of airy flowers. Deadheading will help reduce seedlings. Plants may require staking. USDA zones 3 to 8.

Purple coneflower

Echinacea purpurea
Purple coneflower

    USDA Zones 3 to 8

    Native

    3 to 4 feet

    Zone B

This popular garden plant has showy, 3- to 4-inch, purple-pink petals and bristly orange center cones. It begins blooming early to midsummer and often continues into fall. Plants are shrubby and branching with dark green leaves and fibrous root systems. The plant itself isn't that attractive, so use lower growing plants in front of it to detract. Deadheading doesn't really give more flowers and takes food from the goldfinches. Plus, the seed heads are quite attractive well into winter. Divide only when you have to, since divisions usually don't produce as many flowers. A better way to get more plants is to dig up seedlings in spring, which can be prolific when plants are happy.

Joe-pye weed

Eupatoriadelphus maculatus (Eupatorium maculatum)
Spotted Joe pye weed

    USDA Zones 3 to 8

    Native

    3 to 7 feet tall

    Zone A

Spotted Joe pye weed is a tall, unbranched perennial with whorls of yellowish green leaves up to 8 inches long. Flat-topped, 4- to 5-inch clusters of feathery rose-purple to mauve flower heads appear on top of purple or purple-spotted stems mid- to late summer into fall. The flowers are often fragrant. Plants are late to emerge in spring, so don't forget where they are planted. Spotted Joe pye weed is generally strong of stem and doesn't require staking. Plants can be pinched back when they are about 3 feet tall to produce smaller but fuller flowers or cut back in spring if shorter plants are desired. Bloom will be delayed about a week. Plants do reseed but usually not too prolifically. Until recently, Joe pye weeds were in the same genus as the bonesets, *Eupatorium*. Many sources will still refer to this species as *Eupatorium maculatum*.

    Cultivar: 'Gateway' is a popular cultivar selected for its sturdier, richly colored stems and reduced height, but it still often reaches 6 feet tall and is not really a better choice than the original species.

    Other species: *Conoclinium coelestinum* (*Eupatorium coelestinum*; blue mistflower, hardy ageratum) grows about 2 feet tall and has dense clusters of bright purple flowers late summer into fall. Spreads by seeds; deadhead to reduce amounts. USDA zones 4 to 9. Rain garden zones A, B.

    Eupatorium perfoliatum (common boneset) grows 2 to 4 feet tall with loose clusters of white flowers in summer. The attractive leaves have a wrinkled texture and the bases are fused so stem appears to be pierced by a single long leaf. It spreads via rhizomes and may become weedy. USDA zones 3 to 8. Rain garden zones A, B.

    Eupatoriadelphus dubius (*Eupatorium dubium*; coastal plain Joe pye weed) stays under 4 feet and is hardy in zones 3 to 8.

Queen of the prairie

Plain bottle gentian and
closed bottle gentian

Wild geranium

Eupatorium purpureum (sweetscented Joe pye weed) and *Eupatoriadelphus fistulosus* (hollow Joe pye weed) are two species similar to spotted Joe pye weed, both getting up to 8 feet tall. USDA zones 3 to 9. Rain garden zone A.

Filipendula rubra
Queen of the prairie

> USDA Zones 3 to 7
> Native
> 3 to 7 feet tall
> Zone A

This tall, upright, clump-forming perennial is valued for its foliage as well as its flowers. It has large, astilbe-like panicles of tiny, fragrant, pale pink flowers early to midsummer for about three weeks. The deeply cut, bright green leaves have seven to nine leaflets with an unusually large terminal leaflet. Reddish fruits develop after the flowers. Plants have a taproot and rhizomes and form colonies. The plant will do best in the cooler climate of northern regions rather than areas with hot, dry summers. Flower panicles are best left in place after bloom because deadheading does not extend bloom period. If foliage goes downhill in dry summers it can be cut back hard to promote new growth. Though quite tall, this sturdy plant usually does not need staking.

Gentiana andrewsii
Closed bottle gentian

> USDA Zones 3 to 8
> Native
> 18 to 24 inches tall
> Zone A

Bottle gentian has stunning, deep violet-blue flowers crowded into terminal clusters. The 1-inch, bottle-shaped flowers resemble oversized flower buds even when mature. Individual flowers in a cluster take on various shades of purple as they age. It blooms late summer through fall for about a month. Plants are erect to sprawling with glossy, oval, 4-inch leaves. Multiple stems can emerge from the taproot; otherwise this plant is unbranched and can grow into a good-sized clump with time. Plants seldom need dividing and actually dislike root disturbance. This plant will tolerate higher pH soils.

Other species: *G. alba* (*G. flavida*; plain gentian) has creamy white flowers. USDA zones 3 to 8.

Geranium maculatum
Wild geranium

> USDA Zones 3 to 8
> Native
> 12 to 24 inches tall
> Zone B

Wild geranium has loose clusters of five-petaled, 1-inch-wide flowers rising above pairs of grayish green leaves, each with three to five distinct palmate lobes and coarse teeth. Flowers appear in spring and range from pale to deep magenta-pink to light purple. Deadheading does prolong bloom. Foliage turns a lovely red color in fall. Shelter plants from strong winds.

Other species: There are several cultivars of nonnative, pink-flowering geranium species that do well in rain gardens and are not on invasive lists in any states. These include *G. sanguineium* (bloody cranesbill), USDA zones 4 to 8, and *G. xcatabrigeniensis* (hardy geranium), USDA zones 5 to 8. Avoid planting *G. robertianum* (herb robert), which is invading natural areas.

Sneezeweed

Helenium autumnale
Sneezeweed

> USDA Zones 3 to 8
> Native
> 3 to 5 feet tall
> Zone A

Sneezeweed has abundant daisylike flowers 1 to 2 inches wide with wedge-shaped, bright yellow rays and prominent, domelike, duller yellow center disks. It flowers for a long time beginning in late summer and continuing until the first frost. The bright green leaves are lance-shaped with toothed edges. Plants may need some sort of support to keep from flopping over. Prune back plants to about 12 inches in late May or early June to keep them smaller and more compact. Plants will bloom better if they are divided every three or four years. Sneezeweed does not derive its common name from the effects of its pollen.

Cultivars: Several cultivars are available for more compact growth habit, different colored flowers, and double flowers, but they are not all easy to locate. 'Dakota Gold' stays under 2 feet tall. 'Moerheim Beauty' has bronze-red blossoms. 'Rubinzwerg' (Ruby Dwarf) has ruby red flowers on 2½-foot plants.

Other species: *H. flexuosum* (purplehead sneezeweed) grows 2 to 3 feet tall with clusters of flowers that have drooping yellow petals and much darker brown-purple centers. USDA Zones 5 to 9.

Oxeye

Heliopsis helianthoides
Oxeye

> USDA Zones 3 to 9
> Native
> 3 to 6 feet tall
> Zone A, B

Oxeye has cheery golden yellow flowers starting in early summer and continuing well into fall. The daisylike composite flowers are 2 to 3½ inches across and held erect at the ends of the stiff stems. Leaves are dark green and usually have a rough texture; plants have an overall rather coarse texture. Plants may get floppy; pinch them back in late May to reduce overall height. The named cultivars are less floppy. Oxeye will self-seed, but the shallow-rooted seedlings are easily weeded out. Deadheading will extend the bloom period and prevent seeding, but leave some seed heads for the goldfinches. And plants tend to be short-lived, so you'll want some seedlings.

Cultivars: Several cultivars are available, with 'Summer Sun' being the most popular and easiest to locate. It is more compact than the original species, growing to about 3 feet with large flowers. 'Prairie Sunset' has bright yellow flowers with contrasting orange-red centers. Plants grow to 6 feet with attractive purplish stems and purple-veined leaves. 'Summer Nights' has deep golden yellow flowers with mahogany centers and stems and foliage tinged with red.

Common rose mallow

Hibiscus moscheutos
Common rose mallow

> USDA Zones 4 to 9
> Native
> 4 to 7 feet tall
> Zone A

Common rose mallow is a shrublike perennial with broad, shallowly lobed leaves that grow on erect stalks from a woody crown. Open clusters of 6- to 8-inch white or pinkish flowers with deep red centers appear at the tops of the stems in summer. Flowers only last one day but are produced in abundance for a long time. The dried seed capsules add winter interest. Plants are slow to emerge in spring. Plants are long-lived, and established plants are difficult to divide, so choose a site carefully. They do best in soil with a neutral to slightly alkaline pH.

Other Species: Var. *palustris (H. palustris)* has deep pink flowers and is the form most readily available at nurseries.

H. lasiocarpus (downy rose mallow) has similar flowers, but the leaves are fuzzy and gray green. USDA zones 5 to 9.

Northern blue flag

Iris versicolor
Northern blue flag

> USDA Zones 2 to 8
> Native
> 3 to 4 feet tall
> Zone A

This rhizomatous perennial blooms in late spring, producing several bluish violet flowers on a stout stem among a basal cluster of swordlike, blue-green leaves. The erect, swordlike foliage provides textural contrast throughout the growing season. Plants creep slowly to form nice clumps, which are easily divided every third year for maximum bloom.

Other Species: *I. Cristata* (crested iris) is a charming, smaller species that stays under 8 inches tall. It has violet, occasionally white, flowers in spring. It prefers shadier sites but will do fine in partial sun. USDA zones 4 to 9. Rain garden zone C.

I. fulva (copper iris) grows 2 to 3 feet tall and has beautiful copper red flowers in spring. USDA zones 5 to 9. Rain garden zone A.

I. Sibirica (Siberian iris) is a nonnative species with showy purple flowers on narrower foliage. It grows 3 to 4 feet tall and blooms in late spring. USDA zones 3 to 8. Rain garden zones A, B.

I. virginica (southern blue flag) is similar to northern blue flag but flowers on shorter stems (2 to 3 feet tall), and the new growth has an attractive burgundy tinge. USDA zones 5 to 9. Var. *shrevei* has a more northern range and is hardy through zone 4. It tends to have darker flowers and narrower leaves. Rain garden zone A.

Do not plant yellow-flowered *I. pseudacorus* (yellow flag), an introduced species displacing native species in natural habitats.

'Kobold' dense blazing star

Liatris spicata
Dense blazing star

USDA Zones 3 to 9

Native

2 to 4 feet tall

Zone A, B

Dense blazing star has very showy red-violet to mauve terminal flower spikes midsummer through early fall. The alternating, grasslike leaves increase in size from top to bottom. The root system consists of corms, which occasionally form offsets near the mother plant. The flowers of all *Liatris* species open from the top down and can be one of two general forms: spike or button. All species have strong stems with thin, closely set leaves whorled on the stem. Plants reseed but never become weedy and seldom need dividing. Cut back plants in spring rather than fall so birds can feast on the seed heads. Lower leaves may turn yellow and wither away if conditions become too dry. *Liatris* species may need a little pampering when young, but once established they are easy to maintain.

Cultivars: 'Kobold' is a popular compact cultivar that is less likely to need staking than the original species and is great for perennial borders, cutting gardens, rainwater gardens, and cottage gardens.

Other species: *L. aspera* (rough blazing star) is a button form having clusters of 1-inch, pale purple or pink flowers on short stalks on top of 3- to 5-foot stems. It blooms later (late summer to fall) than most other blazing stars. It will need staking or the support of nearby plants in gardens. USDA zones 3 to 9. Rain garden zone B.

L. ligulistylis (Rocky Mountain blazing star) is a button type with dark violet flowers. It grows 3 to 5 feet tall. USDA zones 3 to 8. Rain garden zone A.

L. pycnostachya (prairie blazing star) is very similar to dense blazing star but grows up to 4 feet tall. USDA zones 3 to 9. Rain garden zone A.

L. scariosa (eastern blazing star) is a button type growing 1 to 4 feet tall. USDA zones 3 to 8. Rain garden zone B.

L. squarrosa (scaly blazing star) is a button type growing 2 to 3 feet tall and blooming earlier than most *Liatris* species. USDA zones 5 to 9. Rain garden zones B, C.

Dense blazing star and prairie blazing star

Michigan lily

Cardinal flower

Ostrich fern

Lilium michiganense
Michigan lily
> USDA Zones 4 to 8
> Native
> 4 to 5 feet tall
> Zone A

Michigan lily has nodding, deep orange flowers with strongly recurved petals flecked with brown in midsummer for about a month. The 2- to 3-inch flowers are held nicely above the stems, and the whorled leaves have smooth margins. A grouping is much more effective than a single plant. Bulbs should be planted 5 to 6 inches deep in fall. This is a slow-spreading stoloniferous plant, with bulbs growing at the ends of the rhizomes. Plants usually need support from staking or neighboring plants.

Lobelia cardinalis
Cardinal flower
> USDA Zones 3 to 9
> Native
> 2 to 4 feet tall
> Zone A

Cardinal flower gets its name from the brilliant rich red flowers that grow in an elongated cluster atop the stems midsummer through early fall. The finely toothed, dark green, lance-shaped leaves reach about 4 inches long. It is a somewhat short-lived, clump-forming perennial. Tubular flowers are two-lipped, with the three lobes of the lower lip appearing more prominent than the two lobes of the upper lip. A dark background will set off the flowers nicely. It definitely takes a bit of coddling, but the cardinal red color in late summer and the hummingbirds it attracts makes the plant worth a little extra effort. It is short-lived, so add seedlings every couple of years or plan to nurse along the offsets that appear in fall. Winter mulch is helpful in colder areas. It will self-seed prolifically in optimum growing conditions. All parts of the plant are toxic if eaten in large quantities

Other species: *L. siphilitica* (blue lobelia) has electric blue flowers arising from the upper leaf axils mid- to late summer. The leafy stalks typically grow 2 to 3 feet tall. It will self-seed prolifically in optimum growing conditions, so it is best used in large rain gardens. It does fine in partial shade. USDA zones 3 to 9. Rain garden zones A, B.

Matteuccia struthiopteris
Ostrich fern
> USDA Zones 3 to 7
> Native
> 2 to 4 feet tall
> Zone A, B
> Slightly acidic soil

Ostrich fern is vase-shaped, with large, plume-like, leathery sterile fronds and smaller fertile fronds that appear in late summer. The fertile fronds become brown and woody in fall and persist through winter, offering interest even into early spring. The young fiddleheads are up early in spring. Ostrich fern does best in a slightly acidic soil. It spreads readily by rhizomes, but it is fairly easy to keep in check. Leaves will scorch if soil becomes dry.

Virginia bluebells

Mertensia virginica
Virginia bluebells

USDA Zones 3 to 9

Native

12 to 24 inches tall

Zone B, C

Virginia bluebells have clusters of pinkish buds that open to showy, drooping clusters of sky blue, trumpet-shaped flowers. The flowers begin opening in midspring and last a long time, but plants usually go dormant soon after blooming. The lettuce-like leaves are oval-shaped, thick-veined, and deep green with smooth margins. They are a showy deep purple color in early spring when they first emerge. The flowers provide a soothing sea of blue for many weeks, filling in spaces before other perennials are up and blooming. Be careful not to dig into dormant clumps. They will self-seed but not to the point of becoming a nuisance.

'Gardenview Scarlet' bee balm

Monarda didyma
Bee balm

USDA Zones 3 to 9

Native

3 to 4 feet tall

Zone A, B

Bee balm has tubular flowers in dense, round, terminal clusters in shades of red. It blooms midsummer through early fall. The foliage is rather coarse, and the stems are square—a mint-family characteristic—branching frequently in the upper half. The root system consists of deep, strongly branched roots and shallow rhizomes, which typically send up multiple leafy stems in a tight cluster, giving plants a bushy appearance. Plantings have a tendency to die out in the middle. Dividing plants every three to four years helps keep them vigorous and reduces their spread. Powdery mildew may be a problem in wet, humid conditions; avoid overhead watering. Plants will self-sow and may become weedy.

Cultivars: There are many cultivars of *M. didyma* available, selected for their various flower colors, more compact growth, and resistance to powdery mildew.

Other species: *M. bradburiana* (eastern bee balm) only grows 1 to 2 feet tall and has pinkish to whitish-purple spotted flowers. It has more resistance to powdery mildew than other species. USDA zones 5 to 8. Rain garden zones B, C.

M. fistulosa (wild bergamot) has soft lavender to pale pink flowers and grows 3 to 4 feet tall. USDA zones 3 to 9. Rain garden zones A, B.

Wild bergamot

Foxglove beardtongue

Penstemon digitalis
Foxglove beardtongue
> USDA Zones 3 to 8
> Native
> 2 to 4 feet tall
> Zones B, C

This clump-forming perennial has white, two-lipped, tubular flowers from midspring to early summer. The flowers appear in panicles atop rigid stems that rise above rosettes of semi-evergreen basal leaves. Leaves are medium green, sometimes with reddish tints. This plant is especially nice massed, but keep in mind its rather short bloom time and uninteresting foliage. Under severe drought conditions the leaves may turn yellow and the plant will wilt. Leaf spots are occasional problems. For a neat appearance, cut bloom stalks once they've turned brown. Plants spread slowly to form dense clumps, and they do reseed but not too prolifically.

Cultivars: 'Husker Red' is a very popular burgundy-leaved selection that greatly extends the season of interest for this species.

'Morris Berd' smooth phlox

Woodland phlox

Phlox glaberrima
Smooth phlox
> USDA Zones 3 to 8
> Native
> 2 to 4 feet tall
> Zone B

This perennial has aromatic, rose to reddish-purple flowers in large, terminal, pyramidal clusters atop stiff, upright stems that seldom need staking and thin, lance-shaped leaves. It blooms late spring into summer. Remove faded flower clusters to prolong bloom and to prevent unwanted self-seeding. It has good resistance to powdery mildew, but spider mites can be a problem, particularly in hot, dry conditions.

Cultivars: 'Morris Berd' has pink flowers with a white center.

Other species: *P. divaricata* (woodland phlox) grows about a foot tall and has clusters of fragrant, pale blue to dark purple-violet flowers from mid- to late spring. The glossy, semi-evergreen foliage spreads at a moderate rate by creeping rhizomes that form loose mats, making this a nice groundcover along the drier outside edges of shady rain gardens. It thrives in partial to full shade in a rich soil. Cut back flower stalks after flowering to keep plants neat. Plants seldom need dividing. USDA hardiness zones 3 to 9. Rain garden zones B, C.

P. maculata (meadow phlox, wild sweet William) grows 2 to 3 feet tall with large, conical clusters of fragrant, pink, lavender, or white flowers in summer. The lance-shaped green leaves are seldom bothered by powdery mildew and look nice all season. Deadheading does prolong the bloom. The plant does best in full sun to light shade. USDA Hardiness zones 3 to 8. Rain garden zone B.

P. pilosa (prairie phlox) grows 1 to 2 feet tall and has showy clusters of white, pink, or lavender flowers. It starts blooming late spring and continues for five weeks or more and may repeat bloom in fall. The leaves are sparsely distributed along the stem, giving plants a fine texture. This taprooted plant occasionally sends up multiple stems from the base. It is not bothered by powdery mildew, but the lower leaves tend to turn yellow and drop off when the plant becomes stressed. Plants can be cut back hard in spring to enhance branching. The plant does reseed but not obnoxiously. Hardiness zones 3 to 9. Rain garden zone C.

P. stolonifera (creeping phlox) stays under a foot tall and makes a nice groundcover plant along the edges of a sunny rain garden. It has lavender or white flowers in spring. It prefers an acidic soil. USDA zones 4 to 9. Rain garden zone C.

'Variegata' obedient plant

Physostegia virginiana
Obedient plant

> USDA Zones 3 to 9
> Native
> 2 to 4 feet tall
> Zones A, B

This perennial has tall, vertical stems lined with narrow, jaggedly toothed leaves. The showy tubular flowers bloom for about six weeks late summer to early fall in somewhat elongated clusters of pinkish, two-lipped, inch-long, snapdragon-like flowers arranged in two rows. A flower spike can be up to 10 inches long, including the unopened buds. The root system consists of a central taproot and rhizomes, which spread aggressively. Plants may need staking, especially if grown in soils with high fertility. Plants can be pruned back in early spring to reduce their overall height. Divide every two to three years to control growth. Deadheading helps improve the plant's appearance and may prolong bloom.

Cultivars: This is a plant that is may be worth seeking out cultivars for because most of them are less invasive than the original species. 'Miss Manners' has bright white flowers and grows about 2 feet tall. 'Olympus Bold' has green and golden variegated foliage and pink flowers on 2½-foot plants. 'Variegata' has pale pink flowers and leaves edged in creamy white. 'Vivid' has vibrant rose-pink flowers on 2- to 2½-foot stems.

Jacob's ladder

Polemonium reptans
Jacob's ladder

> USDA Zones 3 to 8
> Native
> 8 to 16 inches tall
> Zone C

Jacob's ladder is a low-branching, clumping plant with attractive, dark green, pinnately divided leaves. The plants are covered with small sky-blue flowers in terminal clusters held slightly above leaves in spring. Cut bloom stalks to the ground after flowering; foliage will remain attractive all season. Plants do not creep and they seldom need division. The brittle flower stems are easily broken, so any staking should be done before plants flower. This plant prefers a slightly acidic soil in partial shade but can be grown in almost full sun.

Cultivars: 'Stairway to Heaven' has variegated foliage.

Solomon's seal

Gray-headed coneflower

Black-eyed Susan

Polygonatum biflorum
Solomon's seal

> USDA Zones 3 to 8
>
> Native
>
> 1 to 3 feet tall
>
> Zone B

Solomon's seal has greenish yellow flowers that dangle from leaf axils in late spring, but the deep purple fruits that appear later in summer are much more ornamental. They hang from the arching stems and offer great contrast to the foliage, which turns a striking gold color in fall. The 2- to 6-inch, parallel-veined leaves clasp the stem. The graceful, arching stems of giant Solomon's seal bring a strong architectural element to gardens. Tuck clumps here and there for accent. Solomon's seal grows slowly from creeping rhizomes to form natural patches but seldom becomes invasive.

Varieties and Other Species: Var. *commutatum* (great Solomon's seal) is a rare naturally occurring tetraploid form (having more than the regular number of chromosomes). It can grow 6 feet tall or more and is truly spectacular but is difficult to find.

P. odoratum '*Variegatum*' (variegated Solomon's seal) is a nonnative species with showy green leaves with white margins. It grows 1 to 2 feet tall and will spread from rhizomes. USDA zones 3 to 8. Rain garden zone B.

Ratibida pinnata
Gray-headed coneflower

> USDA Zones 3 to 9
>
> Native
>
> 3 to 5 feet tall
>
> Zone B

This hardy, robust perennial has showy, droopy, lemon yellow petals and a grayish brown central disk that can grow up to an inch in diameter and offers interest after the petals fall. The root system is rhizomatous, often forming a dense clump. Blooms are so abundant and plants bloom for a long time, so one plant is often all you'll need. The delicate flowers sway with each passing breeze, bringing movement to a garden. Gray-headed coneflower transplants readily and seldom needs division. Plants reseed abundantly and are difficult to pull once a dense root system is established, so pull seedlings as needed when they are small.

Rudbeckia fulgida
Black-eyed Susan

> USDA Zones 3 to 9
>
> Native
>
> 2 to 3 feet tall
>
> Zones A, B

Black-eyed Susan is well-known by all for its cheery golden yellow rays surrounding a conical cluster of rich brown disc florets. It blooms for a long time, starting midsummer and continuing well into fall. This species is rhizomatous and will form colonies. It also self-sows and produces abundant offsets. The foliage of *Rudbeckia* species is susceptible to several diseases, including Botrytis and powdery mildew. Spacing plants properly and avoiding overhead watering will help keep diseases in check.

Cultivars: 'Goldsturm' is a very popular cultivar of var. *sullivantii* that supposedly has a more compact form. This cultivar appears to be more susceptible to bacterial angular leaf spot, which causes brown or black angular spots on the leaves that can expand to blacken the whole leaf.

Other species: *R. hirta* (black-eyed Susan) grows 1 to 3 feet and is a short-lived perennial. The root system consists of a central taproot and is without rhizomes. Once a planting is established, plants will self-seed to keep the color coming year after year. Deadhead spent flowers to encourage additional bloom and/or to prevent any unwanted seedlings. Plants reproduce entirely by seed, so they never become aggressive vegetatively. USDA hardiness zones 3 to 9. Rain garden zone B.

R. laciniata (cutleaf coneflower, green-headed coneflower) grows 4 to 5 feet tall and has a long bloom time in midsummer. The yellow flowers have light green centers. USDA Hardiness zones 3 to 9. Rain garden zone A.

R. maxima (great coneflower) grows 3 to 4 feet tall and has a basal clump of huge paddle-shaped leaves. The flowers have drooping petals and dark brown centers. USDA zones 5 to 9. Rain garden zone A.

R. subtomentosa (sweet coneflower) blooms later, grows taller than most other species, 3 to 5 feet, and is a little more sunflower-like in appearance with its dark brown-purple center disks and yellow rays. The gray-green, sweet-scented leaves form large bushy clumps, but the plant is not rhizomatous. Pinch plants back lightly in spring to reduce their height and lankiness. USDA zones 3 to 9. Rain garden zone A.

R. triloba (brown-eyed Susan) can get up to 5 feet in height. The buttonlike flowers are smaller than other species but very abundant and have jet-black centers. This plant will reseed prolifically when it is happy in moist soils. Deadhead spent flowers to encourage additional bloom and/or to prevent any unwanted seedlings. USDA zones 3 to 9. Rain garden zones A, B.

Wild petunia

Ruellia humilis
Wild petunia

USDA Zones 4 to 9
Native
1 to 2 feet tall
Zone C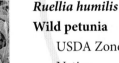

This charming perennial has tubular, bell-shaped flowers up to 3 inches in diameter that are a lovely lavender or light purple color. It blooms for a long time beginning in early summer and continuing sporadically until the first frost. The olive green leaves and the stems are hairy. The root system is fibrous and plants spread to become bushy clumps. Plants are slow to emerge in spring. Deadhead flowers if you don't want an overabundance of seedlings.

Cup plant

Silphium perfoliatum
Cup plant

> USDA Zones 3 to 9
>
> Native
>
> 3 to 8 feet tall
>
> Zone A, B

There is nothing small about plants in this genus, and they should only be used in large rain gardens where they can be left undisturbed. Cup plant has leaves that encircle tall stems and form cups that collect dew and become drinking fountains for birds, including humming-birds. The 3-inch yellow flowers bloom in branched clusters just above the leaves in mid- to late summer. The plant takes a little more shade than other species. A rainstorm with strong winds can topple blooming plants. Various birds, especially goldfinches, are very fond of the seeds. The dense colonies provide good cover for birds, which often lurk among the leaves during the heat of the day searching for insects or pausing to rest.

Other species: *S. laciniatum* (compass plant) grows 3 to 8 feet tall and has lemon yellow, sunflower-like flowers up to 5 inches across at the ends of branched, hairy, sticky stems midsummer for about five weeks. The 12- to 18-inch, showy, cut-leaf blades orient themselves horizontally in a north-south direction to avoid the intense rays of midday sun. The taproot can extend 15 feet deep, and plants are said to live up to 100 years. Established clumps are difficult to divide or move, so choose a site carefully. The plant likes full sun. The foliage turns brown after flowering, so you need to plant something in front of it. USDA zones 3 to 9. Rain garden zones A, B.

S. terebinthinaceum (prairie dock) grows 4 to 8 feet tall and is noteworthy for the large paddlelike leaves that have a tropical look. A tall, naked flowering stalk emerges from this leafy rosette and sports a panicle of yellow flowers, each up to 3 inches across. The bloom period is late summer to early fall for about a month, a bit later than other *Silphium* species. The stout taproot can go down 12 feet and may form offsets a short distance away from the mother plant. This plant likes full sun. USDA zones 3 to 9. Rain garden zones A, B.

Showy goldenrod

Solidago speciosa
Showy goldenrod

> USDA Zones 3 to 9
>
> Native
>
> 2 to 5 feet tall
>
> Zone B

This plant is very showy while in bloom from late summer through fall. The showy inflorescence is up to 1 foot long, consisting of an erect panicle of small, bright yellow, compound flowers. The flowering stems are held erect or curve upward, unlike most goldenrod flowers that flop down. The plant is rather coarse when not in bloom with alternating leaves up to 6 inches long and 1½ inches wide. The root system is fibrous and rhizomatous, occasionally forming vegetative offsets. Goldenrods have been wrongly accused of causing hay fever, which is actually an allergic reaction to wind-borne pollen from other plants like ragweed. Cut back hard after flowering if reseeding is a problem. Plan to divide plants every two to three years to control growth. Plants may topple over if they are given excessive moisture or fertilizer.

Other species: *S. rigida (Oligoneuron rigidum)* also grows about 2 to 5 feet tall. It has attractive flattened flower panicles and nice gray-green, downy leaves that turn dusty rose in fall. It can be used in large rainwater gardens, where it will self-sow but is usually not too invasive. Hardiness Zones 3 to 9. Rain garden zone B.

There are also several other species that can be considered for use in rain garden zone B.

New England aster

Symphyotrichum novae-angliae
New England aster
> USDA Zones 3 to 8
> Native
> 3 to 6 feet tall
> Zones A, B

New England aster's showy flowers have petals ranging from violet to pink to white surrounding yellow centers and can be up to 2 inches wide. The plant blooms from late summer through fall. Mature plants have woody, fibrous root systems and form thick clumps after a few years. The tall stems of the species can become top heavy when in bloom and usually need some type of support. Cut plants back to about a foot in spring to promote bushier plants. Divide plants in spring every third year to promote vigorous growth. Plants are susceptible to leaf spots, rusts, and mildew, problems that can leave lower leaves in bad shape by flowering time but usually do no permanent harm. Plants can be cut to the ground after flowering if they look too unsightly. *Aster* species have been reclassified and most North American species are now in *Symphyotrichum*. The species can be a bit coarse for front-yard rain gardens, but the many cultivars are good choices where a more-refined look is desired.

Cultivars: There are dozens of cultivars of New England aster available, mainly selected for more compact growth habit, better lower leaf retention, and earlier and longer bloom time than the origin species. Here are a few of the more commonly available selections to consider: 'Andenken an Alma Potschke,' usually sold simply as 'Alma Potschke,' is covered in bright rose-pink flowers on 3- to 4-foot plants. 'Harrington's Pink' has unique light salmon-pink flowers but can grow up to 5 feet tall. 'Hella Lacy' grows 3 to 4 feet tall with violet-blue flowers. 'Honeysong Pink' grows about 3½ feet tall and has pink petals with bright yellow disks. 'Purple Dome' is a naturally dense dwarf cultivar (18 to 24 inches) with semi-double, deep purple flowers. 'Roter Stern' (Red Star) stays about 15 inches tall and has red flowers. 'September Ruby' has deep ruby red flowers on floppy, 3- to 5-foot plants. 'Wedding Lace' grows 4 feet tall with whitish flowers.

Other species: There are many other asters that can be considered for use in rain garden zone B. They range in height from 1 to 6 feet or more and have flowers in shades of purple and white. The list includes *Eurybia macrophyllus* (bigleaf aster), *S. chilense* (Pacific aster), *S. dumosum* (rice button aster), *S. ericoides* (white heath aster), *S. laevis* (smooth aster), *S. novae-belgii* (New York aster), *S. oblongifolium* (aromatic aster), *S. oolentangiense* (skyblue aster), *S. patens* (late purple aster), *S. sericeum* (western silver aster), *S. subspicatum* (Douglas aster), and *S. turbinellum* (prairie aster).

Foamflower

Spiderwort

Ironweed

Tiarella cordifolia
Foamflower

> USDA Zones 3 to 9
> Native
> 3 to 10 inches tall
> Zone C

Foamflower gets its name from the frothy conical clusters of white flowers that are sometimes flushed with pink. They appear in spring. The handsome maple-leaf foliage is attractive all summer long, turning a beautiful red in autumn. Plants spread by trailing stolons and will eventually form a weed-smothering mat of foliage. Remove unwanted rooted runners at any time to keep plants from spreading too far. Foamflower may need supplemental water during dry periods. It does best in a slightly acidic soil.

Other species: *T. trifoliata* (threeleaf foamflower), native in the Pacific Northwest, is daintier and clumpier in its growth habit. USDA zones 4 to 8.

Tradescantia ohiensis
Spiderwort

> USDA Zones 3 to 9
> Native
> 1½ to 2½ feet tall
> Zones A, B, C

This perennial has gray- or blue-green, straplike leaves up to 15 inches long and 1 inch wide, tending to bend downward toward the middle—think daylilies when not in bloom. The light violet to blue-violet flowers occur in a small cluster at the top of the plant. Each flower is about an inch across with three rounded petals. Flowers open in the morning and close by afternoon in sunny weather, remaining open longer on cloudy days. Plants can bloom from late spring right into fall, with only a few flowers in bloom at the same time. The root system is thick, fleshy, and fibrous, sending off occasional offshoots nearby. Spiderworts can be a bit aggressive, but the intense blue color and long bloom time make them worth a little effort. Plants will reseed and the seedlings can be difficult to pull. Plants can be cut back to 6 to 12 inches in midsummer to keep them neater and reduce unwanted seedlings.

Other species: *T. virginiana* (Virginia spiderwort) is a similar species that likes more shade. USDA zones 3 to 9.

Vernonia fasciculata
Ironweed

> USDA Zones 3 to 9
> Native
> 3 to 5 feet tall
> Zone A

This butterfly-attracting, but somewhat coarse, perennial has long, narrow leaves along the thick stems. The central stem terminates in a flat-topped cluster of magenta flowers from late summer to early fall for about a month. The root system is spreading and fibrous. Bunched ironweed is best used in large rain gardens where it offers a strong vertical presence. Pinch back stems in late May to keep plants more compact. Unpinched plants may need staking or support of some kind.

Other species: *V. noveboracensis* (New York ironweed) is similar but can grow even taller, up to 8 feet, and the flowers are in looser heads. USDA zones 3 to 9.

Culver's root

Veronicastrum virginicum
Culver's root

> USDA Zones 3 to 9
> Native
> 3 to 6 feet tall
> Zone A

This perennial is upright and unbranched except near the inflorescence. The dark green, whorled leaves give the plant a horizontal effect that contrasts with the strongly vertical spires of white or pale lavender, candelabra-like flowers. Culver's root starts blooming in midsummer and continues for about a month. Unfortunately the pretty white flowers rapidly turn brown. The root system consists of a central taproot and some rhizomes. Culver's root forms clumps as it ages but is not overly aggressive. Plants don't usually need staking unless they are grown in too much shade. Plants usually take several years to establish in a garden. The leaves may turn yellowish green in bright sunlight or during a drought; otherwise they normally appear healthy and are not often bothered by disease.

Golden alexanders

Zizia aurea
Golden alexanders

> USDA Zones 4 to 8
> Native
> 1 to 3 feet tall
> Zone B, C

Golden alexanders has cheery yellow, 3-inch umbels for about a month in late spring to early summer. The shiny compound leaves are trifoliate, with leaflets up to 3 inches long. The root system is a dense cluster of coarse fibrous roots. The flattened heads of yellow flowers are a bright accent in a spring garden and the delicate foliage looks nice as well. It will weave its way through other plants. Individual plants may be short-lived, but they will self-sow to maintain the population. Foliage tends to depreciate as the summer progresses.

Siberian bugloss

Bleeding heart

Royal catchfly

Other Perennials to Consider, listed with their Rain Garden Zones

Acorus calamus (calamus)* A

Acorus gramineus (grassy-leaved sweet flag) A

Agastache foeniculum (anise hyssop)* B

Alchemilla mollis (lady's mantle) B, C

Aralia nudicaulis (wild sarsaparilla)* B

Aralia racemosa (American spikenard)* B

Arisaema triphyllum (Jack in the pulpit)* B, C

Astilbe chinensis 'Pumila' B, C

Astilbe xarendsii cultivars (astilbes) B

Begonia grandis (hardy begonia) A, B

Blephilia ciliata (horsemint)* C

Brunnera macrophylla (Siberian bugloss) B, C

Caltha palustris (yellow marsh marigold)* A, B

Camassia species (camases)* A, B

Campanula rotundifolia (bluebell)* C

Dalea purpurea (purple prairie clover)* B, C

Dianthus gratianopolitanus (cheddar pink) C

Dicentra eximia (fringed bleeding heart)* B, C.

Dicentra spectabilis (bleeding heart) B, C

Dodecatheon species (shooting stars)* C

Epimedium xyoungianum (barrenwort) C

Eryngium yuccifolium (rattlesnake master)* B

Euphorbia corollata (flowering spurge)* C

Fragaria species (wild strawberries)* C

Gaillardia xgrandiflora (hybrid blanketflower)* B, C

Galium odoratum (sweet woodruff) C

Gaultheria procumbens (eastern teaberry, wintergreen)* C

Gaultheria shallon (salal)* C

Geum triflorum (prairie smoke)* C

Helianthus angustifolius (swamp sunflower)* A

Helleborus species (hellebores) C

Hepatica species (hepaticas)* C

Heuchera species (alumroots)* B, C

Heuchera cultivars (heucheras) B, C

Hosta cultivars (hostas) B, C

Hylotelephium spectabile (*Sedum spectabile*; showy stonecrop) B, C

Leucanthemum x superbum (shasta daisy) B

Ligularia cultivars (ligularias) A

Maianthemum canadense (Canada mayflower)* B, C

Maianthemum racemosum (false Solomon's seal)* B, C

Mimulus ringens (Allegheny monkey flower)* A

Pachysandra procumbens (Allegheny-spurge)* C

Paeonia hybrids (peonies) B, C

Alumroot

Showy stonecrop

Parthenium integrifolium (wild quinine)* B, C

Perovskia atriplicifolia (Russian sage) B

Primula species (primroses) C

Pycnanthemum species (mountain mints)* B

Rodgersia pinnata (Rodger's flower) A, B

Salvia lyrata (lyreleaf sage)* A, B

Salvia xsupberba (hybrid sage) B, C

Sedum ternatum (woodland stonecrop)* C

Silene regia (royal catchfly)* B

Sisyrinchium species (blue-eyed grasses)* C

Solidago species (goldenrods)* B

Stachys byzantina (lamb's ears) C

Stylophorum diphyllum (celandine poppy)* B

Tellima grandiflora (fringecups)* B

Thalictrum aquilegifolium (columbine meadow-rue) B

Thalictrum dasycarpum (purple meadow-rue)* A, B

Thermopsis villosa (Carolina lupine)* B

Thymus serpyllum (creeping thyme) C

Tolmiea menziesii (youth on age)* C

Trollius xcultorum (European globeflower) A, B

Verbena hastata (blue vervain, swamp verbena)* A

Viola labradorica (Labrador violet)* C

Viola pedata (birdfoot violet)* C

Waldsteinia fragarioides (barren strawberry)* C

*North American natives

Other Ferns to Consider, listed with their Rain Garden Zones

Blechnum spicant (deer fern)* A, B

Dennstaedtia punctilobula (hayscented fern)* A, B

Deparia acrostichoides (silvery spleenwort)* A, B

Dryopteris cristata (crested wood fern)* A, B

Dryopteris marginalis (marginal wood fern)* B

Onoclea sensibilis (sensitive fern)* A, B

Osmunda cinnamomea (cinnamon fern)* A, B

Osmunda claytoniana (interrupted fern)* A, B

Osmunda regalis (royal fern)* A, B

Polystichum acrostichoides (Christmas fern)* B, C

Polystichum munitum (western sword fern)* B

Thelypteris noveboracensis (New York fern)* A

Thelypteris palustris (eastern marsh fern)* A

Sensitive fern

*North American natives

Grasses and Grasslike Plants

Big bluestem

Andropogon gerardii
Big bluestem

> USDA Zones 3 to
> Native
> 4 to 8 feet tall
> Zones A, B

Big bluestem is an upright, clump-forming, warm-season grass with blue-green stems topped with fingerlike racemes of fruiting clusters. The silvery white flowers, which resemble upside-down turkey feet, appear in midsummer but really stand out by late summer. The fall foliage color is an attractive bronzy reddish brown. Big bluestem is long-lived, so choose a site carefully. Many insects feed on the leaves, songbirds enjoy the seeds, and birds and mammals use it for nesting and winter cover. Mow or cut back in spring.

Carex pensylvanica
Pennsylvania sedge

> USDA Zones 3 to 8
> Native
> 6 to 10 inches tall
> Zone C

Pennsylvania sedge

This sedge spreads by stolons, forming large colonies of loose tufts of fine-textured bright green leaves that arch over and provide very early color in spring. Brownish flower spikes appear in mid- to late spring. Plants spread slowly, so if you want a solid groundcover place clumps as close together as you can afford to. Plants can be divided anytime during the growing season to increase your numbers.

Other Species: *C. muskingumensis* (palm sedge) grows 2 to 3 feet tall and has wide, straplike, light green leaves that resemble palm fronds. Grow it in sun or shade. The creeping rhizomes spread slowly to form an effective groundcover. USDA zones 4 to 9. Rain gardens zones A, B.

C. stricta (tussock sedge) forms a dense, 2-foot clump of long, slender leaves that arch outward, creating a symmetrical fountain-like effect. It grows in sun or shade. As the plants develop, they form vertical-sided columns on which they grow, raising them above their surroundings and further enhancing their distinctive appearance. USDA zones 3 to 8. Rain garden zones A, B.

Other native sedges to consider for rain garden zone A in sun to partial shade: *C. crinita* (fringed sedge), *C. grayi* (Gray's sedge), and *C. vulpinoidea* (fox sedge).

Chasmanthium latifolium
Northern sea oats

> USDA Zones 4 to 9
> Native
> 3 to 4 feet tall
> Zones A, B

Tufted hairgrass

Blue oat grass

Rush flower

Northern sea oats is a clump-forming, upright grass distinguished by its flat, drooping seed heads that flutter in the slightest breeze. The grass emerges green but turns purplish bronze by late summer and brown in winter. It combines nicely with many perennials. The foliage may turn yellow if soil is lacking in nitrogen. The tough, woody rhizomes are hard to divide. It is one grass that is easy to grow from seed, and it will reseed in rain gardens.

Deschampsia caespitosa
Tufted hairgrass

> USDA Zones 2 to 7
>
> Native
>
> 3 to 4 feet tall
>
> Zone B

This cool-season clumping grass forms tight basal tufts that grow about 1 foot tall and eventually spread about 2 feet wide. During summer it produces large, open panicles of glistening silver-tinted flower heads that reach about 3 feet in height. The panicles turn yellowish tan as the seed ripens and remain attractive through much of the winter. This is a wonderful native grass for cooler climates, but it is not as well-suited to southern areas. It offers the beauty of an ornamental grass long before any of the warm-season grasses are showy. The fine-textured flowers and seed heads are especially effective when backlit or set off by a dark background. Cut back plants in late fall or very early spring. Plants may self-sow in optimum conditions but rarely become a nuisance.

Helictotrichon sempervirens
Blue oat grass

> USDA Zones 4 to 8
>
> Nonnative
>
> 2 to 3 feet tall
>
> Zone C

Blue oat grass is a clump-forming, cool-season grass with very narrow, spiky, steel blue leaf blades that form a rounded clump. Spikelets of bluish-brown flowers arranged in open, one-sided panicles arching at the tip appear on erect stems rising well above the foliage clump in late spring and turn a golden wheat color by fall. It is a nice accent plant where the blue foliage offers contrast in a sea of green. Cut back in late winter.

Juncus effusus
Common rush

> USDA Zones 3 to 9
>
> Native
>
> 2 to 4 feet tall
>
> Zone A

Rushes have rounded stems and interesting flowers. Common rush is an upright, clump-forming rush with bright to dark green stems that often stay green through the winter. Flowers appear at the tips of the slender stems. Rushes offer interesting contrast in rain gardens with their spiky forms and unusual spring flowers. They are slow to establish and can go several years without dividing but will eventually form large clumps if they are happy. Divide in spring when needed.

Cultivars: Several cultivars have been selected for curly stems, foliage color, and variegation. 'Spiralis,' 'Gold Strike,' and 'Unicorn' are among the most readily available.

Other species: There are many species of native rushes that can be considered for Zone A in the sunny rain garden. Here are a few that are easier to find: *J. acuminatus* (tapertip rush), *J. patens* (spreading rush), and *J. tenuis* (poverty rush).

Switchgrass

Panicum virgatum
Switchgrass
> USDA Zones 3 to 9
> Native
> 3 to 6 feet tall
> Zone A, B

This warm-season clumping grass grows from a dense crown of congested rhizomes. The 1- to 2-foot long green, blue-green, or silver leaves are sometimes tinged with red toward the tapering tip. Fall color is golden yellow to deep burgundy. The seeds are produced in open, billowy panicles in late summer. There is a lot of natural variation in switchgrass, which has helped lead to the large number of cultivars selected. The open flower panicles look best when viewed against a dark background. The dense foliage stands up well in winter and offers great winter interest outside. Allow 2 to 3 feet between plants, as clumps become large. Plants are fairly slow to spread, but division will be needed every four years or so to keep plants under control in gardens. Most cultivars do not produce a lot of seeds, but the species will self-sow on open, moist soils.

Cultivars: There are many selections of switchgrass available, and they are usually better choices for small rain gardens because they tend to reseed and spread at a much lower rate than the origin species. Choose a cultivar based on its fall color, the degree of blue in its foliage, its height, or its ability to resist lodging and stay upright. 'Amber Wave' stays less than 4 feet in height. 'Dallas Blues' has broad steel blue to gray green foliage and huge purple flower panicles. 'Heavy Metal' has metallic blue foliage that turns yellow in fall. 'Northwind' is very sturdy and upright. 'Rotstrahlbusch' has good red fall color. 'Shenandoah' has reddish purple foliage color by midsummer and a distinct reddish cast to the 3-inch flower heads.

Little bluestem

Schizachyrium scoparium
Little bluestem
> USDA Zones 3 to 9
> Native
> 2 to 4 feet tall
> Zone B, C

This attractive clumping grass has light green to blue foliage in summer, turning golden to reddish brown in fall and remaining very showy all through winter. Flowering begins in late summer, but the thin flower heads really aren't noticeable until they turn to attractive silvery-white seed heads. The fluffy seed heads and crimson-colored foliage are extremely showy in the fall landscape. Little bluestem is among the best native grasses for fall color, and its small size makes it easy to use in most rain gardens. Remember, however, being a warm-season grass it won't "green up" until late spring. Cut back clumps in late winter. It will reseed.

Cultivars: The species is quite attractive and well-behaved, but there are some cultivars to consider. 'The Blues' is the most popular, selected for its good blue-green foliage color.

Indian grass

Sorghastrum nutans
Indian grass
> USDA Zones 3 to 9
>
> Native
>
> 3 to 5 feet tall
>
> Zone B

This warm-season grass develops from a loose clump of thick rhizomes. It produces showy copper-colored flowers in late summer that have large, dangling yellow-orange anthers. Its fall foliage color is golden yellow to dark orange, contrasting nicely with the golden brown silky tassels of the seeds. When its large size can be accommodated, Indian grass makes a nice addition to rain gardens, where it provides a strong vertical accent. It provides a nice back-drop for lower-growing forbs. Cut back plants in late winter. It is not overly aggressive.

Cultivars: Several cultivars have been selected, most for their deeper blue foliage and upright growth habit. 'Sioux Blue' is the best known and most widely available.

Other Grasses and Grasslike Plants to Consider, Listed with Their Rain Garden Zones

Prairie dropseed

> *Bouteloua curtipendula* (sideoats grama)* B, C
>
> *Calamagrostis xacutiflora* (feather reed grass) A, B
>
> *Calamagrostis canadensis* (blue joint)* A, B
>
> *Elymus canadensis* (Canadian wild rye)* B, C
>
> *Equisetum hyemale* (horsetail)* A
>
> *Pennisetum alopecouriodes* (fountain grass) B, C
>
> *Pennisetum orientale* (fountain grass) B
>
> *Scirpus* species (bulrushes)* A, B
>
> *Spartina* species (cordgrasses)* A, B
>
> *Sporobolus heterolepis* (prairie dropseed)* C

> *North American natives

Shrubs and Small Trees

'Regent' serviceberry

Amelanchier alnifolia
Saskatoon serviceberry

> USDA Zones 2 to 6
> Native
> 6 to 15 feet tall, 5 to 10 feet wide
> Zone A, B ☀ ◪

These deciduous shrubs have small white flowers in early spring before the leaves fully emerge. Flowers turn to green berries that mature into dark purple fruit in early summer. The fruit attracts wildlife and can also be used for jams, jellies, pies, and wine—if you can keep it from the birds. Remove some of the older stems each year in late winter to keep plants vigorous and producing more fruit. Renew overgrown shrubs with hard pruning. Root suckers are common, and if not removed, will result in a shrubby growth habit for the plant. Serviceberries usually have good fall color and the bark is silvery gray.

Cultivars: 'Regent' is a popular selection that stays 4 to 6 feet tall and wide.

Other species: *A. laevis* (smooth juneberry, Alleghany serviceberry) is a single or multi-stemmed small tree or large shrub growing 25 to 40 feet tall and 15 to 25 feet wide. Leaves are purple in early spring, turning green in summer and red-orange in fall. USDA Hardiness Zones 3 to 8. Rain garden zones A, B.

A. x grandiflora (apple serviceberry) is a naturally occurring hybrid of *A. arborea* and *A. laevis*. It is an excellent small clump or single-trunked tree growing to about 25 feet. Several cultivars have been selected for their good fall color and interesting growth habits. Good choices include 'Autumn Brilliance,' 'Robin Hill,' 'Princess Diana,' and 'Strata.' USDA Zones 4 to 8. Rain garden zones A, B.

American hornbeam

Carpinus caroliniana
American hornbeam

> USDA Zones 3 to 9
> Native
> 20 to 30 feet tall, 15 to 20 feet wide
> Zones B ☀ ◪ ●

Also known as blue beech, American hornbeam is a bushy small tree or shrub with a spreading irregular crown. The beautiful muscle-like bark is bluish gray, smooth, and sometimes marked with dark brown horizontal bands. Slender brownish catkins dangle from branches in early to mid-April. Leaves are dark green in summer, changing to a beautiful orange to red to reddish purple in autumn. Small nutlets hang in clusters and turn brown, adding interest in fall and winter as well as food for birds. American hornbeam is somewhat difficult to transplant; move balled-and-burlapped or container-grown plants in early spring. Plants can be shaped with selective pruning to form a single trunk that will showcase the interesting bark. Without pruning, plants will send up suckers from the base and become shrubby in appearance. This plant does best in a slightly acidic soil.

Buttonbush

Cephalanthus occidentalis

Buttonbush

> USDA Zones 4 to 10
>
> Native
>
> 3 to 8 feet tall, 3 to 6 feet wide
>
> Zones A, B

Buttonbush is a low-branched shrub with smooth, gray-green bark. Its attractive medium-green leaves nicely set off the white flowers, which are borne in a 1-inch globe with protruding pistils. It blooms when few other plants are in flower, from late July into August. The flowers have a musky, sweet scent. Bright red fruits form in autumn. Pruning is usually not necessary, but may be done in early spring to shape. If plants become unmanageable, they may be cut back near to the ground in early spring to revitalize; they'll grow to 3 feet tall by midsummer and still flower on the new growth. Buttonbush often dies back to the ground after a severe winter in zones 4 and 5.

Eastern redbud

Cercis canadensis

Eastern redbud

> USDA Zones 4 to 9
>
> Native
>
> 15 to 30 feet tall, 20 to 25 feet wide
>
> Zone B

This small spreading tree has large (4-inch) heart-shaped leaves that start out reddish purple, turn bluish green in summer, and yellow in autumn. The showy purple-pink flowers appear in early spring before the leaves. Flat, peapod-like fruits appear in early autumn and persist through winter. Bark on mature trees is reddish brown to black and furrowed. Redbud, often grown as a clump tree, offers color and interest all year round but is sensitive to salt, so keep it away from salted walks and roads. Best flowering occurs on trees four years old and older.

Cultivars: 'Alba' (var. *alba*) has pure white flowers. 'Forest Pansy' has new leaves that are scarlet becoming maroon as they mature. 'Flame' ('Plena') has double pink flowers and seldom sets fruit. 'Royal White' has large white flowers. 'Silver Cloud' has leaves variegated with pink and white and grows 12 feet tall and wide.

Summersweet

Clethra alnifolia

Summersweet

> USDA Zones 4 to 9
>
> Native
>
> 3 to 8 feet tall, 4 to 6 feet wide
>
> Zones A, B

A slender, upright, slowly spreading, deciduous shrub with fluffy terminal spikes of extremely fragrant white flowers, summersweet blooms on current season's growth for 4 to 6 weeks in mid- to late summer. The glossy, dark green leaves turn a striking yellow in autumn, and flower spikes give way to dark brown seed capsules that persist into winter. One of the few summer-blooming shrubs that will grow in partial shade, it spreads slowly by rhizomes.

Gray dogwood

Cornus amomum

Silky dogwood

> USDA Zones 4 to 8
>
> Native
>
> 3 to 10 feet tall, 3 to 6 feet wide
>
> Zones A, B

There are several *Cornus* species that do well in rain gardens. While silky dogwood does not rank at the top of the list for showiness, it is very well suited to rain garden use. It has 2-inch white flower clusters, porcelain-blue berries, and purple-red fall color. All dogwoods are good for attracting wildlife. Possible disease problems include leaf spot, crown canker, blights, root rot, and powdery mildew. These diseases result in unattractive foliage in late summer and early fall but are not serious enough to kill plants.

Other species: *C. alternifolia* (pagoda dogwood) grows 20 to 25 feet tall and up to 25 feet wide as a small tree or large shrub. It has attractive horizontal tiers of branches, giving it a layered appearance. The deep green leaves are heavily veined and turn reddish in fall. Small, creamy-white, musk-scented flowers appear in 3- to 5-inch clusters from late May to early June. The fruit is green and berrylike, turning to white to blue to nearly black on red stalks. Does best in light shade. USDA zones 3 to 8. Rain garden zone B.

C. racemosa (gray dogwood) grows 8 to 12 feet tall and up to 10 feet wide. The attractive gray stems support creamy-white flowers in May; they are followed by showy white fruit borne on red pedicels in late summer. Birds eat the fruit, but the showy red pedicels persist, contrasting nicely with snow. This plant grows best in full sun but is tolerant of partial shade. It spreads slowly by underground stems but can be successfully grown as a specimen tree with persistent pruning. It has good red fall color. USDA zones 3 to 8. Rain garden zone B.

C. sericea (red osier dogwood) grows 8 to 10 feet tall and almost as wide. It has deep red stems and twigs that are showy in winter; creamy-white flowers in spring followed by attractive white fruit; and maroon-colored fall leaves. It spreads by layering when the lower stems touch or lie along the ground and can form dense thickets in the right conditions. Younger stems have the brightest color, so prune out oldest stems each spring to encourage new growth. Overgrown plants can be cut back to about 6 inches in spring. It is the same plant as *C. stolonifera*. 'Cardinal' has bright cherry-red stems. 'Isanti' has a compact habit, growing to about 6 feet tall, and good stem color. USDA zones 2 to 7. Rain garden zones A, B.

Witchhazel

Hamamelis virginiana

Witchhazel

> USDA Zones 4 to 8
>
> Native
>
> 10 to 20 feet tall, 10 to 15 feet wide
>
> Zone B

This deciduous shrub is the last shrub to bloom in autumn, producing golden-yellow flowers that are slightly fragrant. The flowers take a back seat to the wonderful golden-yellow fall leaf color. This open, multi-stemmed shrub has a tighter growth habit when grown in more light. Its branches have a zigzag pattern. Witchhazel doesn't really have a lot to offer ornamentally until it blooms in fall, so plan to surround it with spring- and summer-blooming plants to distract the eye. It can be pruned into a small, wide-spreading tree. Rejuvenate overgrown shrubs with heavy pruning in early spring.

Other species: *H. vernalis* (spring witchhazel) is the spring-blooming version, with flowers appearing very early, often in late winter while snow is still on the ground. They are quite a bit showier because there is little else blooming at this time, and they are not hidden by leaves. The bush stays a little smaller in size, usually only growing 6 to 10 feet tall, but it will spread more. It does best with a slightly acidic soil. USDA zones 4 to 8. Rain garden zone B.

Oakleaf hydrangea

Hydrangea quercifolia
Oakleaf hydrangea

> USDA Zones 5 to 9
>
> Native
>
> 6 to 8 feet tall, 6 to 8 feet wide
>
> Zone B

This beautiful shrub offers interest year round. It has conical clusters of white flowers that start blooming in late spring and slowly turn pinkish purple with age. The distinctive, deeply lobed, oak-like leaves turn attractive shades of bronze, crimson or purple in autumn. Mature stems exfoliate to reveal a rich brown inner bark, which is attractive in winter. The heavy flowers may droop, especially after rain.

Other species: *H. arborescens* (smooth hydrangea) grows 3 to 5 feet tall and up to 8 feet wide. It has lacecap flowers arranged in symmetrical, rounded heads 4 to 6 inches across and dark green leaves. It blooms on the current season's wood off and on throughout the summer. In cold winter climates, it is perhaps best grown as an herbaceous perennial and cut back to the ground in late winter. It will tolerate full sun in northern rain gardens but needs some shade in southern areas. 'Annabelle' is a popular selection that has much larger flowers than the origin species. USDA zones 4 to 9. Rain garden zone B.

Winterberry

Ilex verticillata
Winterberry

> USDA Zones 3 to 9
>
> Native
>
> 6 to 10 feet tall, 6 to 10 feet wide
>
> Zones A, B

A deciduous holly, winterbetty loses its leaves in winter. With leaves that vary from flat to shiny on the upper surface, its autumn color is not especially showy, but from late fall through winter, winterberry steps into the spotlight with an outstanding display of bright red berries that persist even after the leaves have fallen. Berries are only produced on female plants. Plant one male plant in close proximity to three to five female plants to ensure good pollination and subsequent fruit set. Little pruning is needed, but it does need an acidic soil.

Cultivars: Several cultivars have been selected. Most are females that require a male pollinator to set fruit. 'Afterglow' features smaller, glossy green leaves and large orange-red berries maturing to orange. 'Cacapon' stays at 6 feet and has bright red fruits. 'Red Sprite' (also known as 'Compacta') is a popular dwarf maturing to only 3 to 4 feet tall. 'Shaver' has large clusters of red-orange berries. Use 'Jim Dandy' to pollinate all four cultivars. 'Winter Red' has a good growth habit and profuse bright red fruits that consistently persist into winter; 'Southern Gentleman' is a good pollinator for 'Winter Red.'

Other species: *I. decidua* (possum haw) is a similar deciduous species that does better in southern gardens. It grows 7 to 15 feet tall and the glossy, dark green leaves turn a dull purplish green to yellow in autumn. USDA zones 6 to 9. Rain garden zones A, B.

I. Glabra (inkberry) is a slow-growing, upright-rounded, stoloniferous, broadleaf evergreen shrub. It typically matures to 5 to 8 feet tall, and can spread by root suckers to form colonies. It has spineless, flat, glossy, dark green leaves with smooth margins with several marginal teeth near the apex. Leaves usually remain attractive in winter unless temperatures dip well below zero. Inconspicuous greenish white flowers appear in spring. Pollinated female flowers give way to pea-sized, jet black, berry-like fruits that mature in early fall and persist throughout winter to early spring unless consumed by birds. Cultivars typically have better form (more compact, less open, less leggy and less suckering) than the original species. This bush does best in full sun to partial shade in USDA zones 5 to 9. Rain garden zones A, B.

I. opaca (American holly) is a small, evergreen tree with a narrow, pyramidal crown. It grows slowly to 15 to 30 feet tall and has spiny-toothed, dull green leaves. Inconspicuous greenish white flowers of both male and female trees appear in spring. Pollinated female flowers produce red berries, which ripen in October and persist throughout winter. USDA zones 5 to 9. Rain garden zone B.

I. vomitoria (yaupon) is a thicket-forming, broadleaf evergreen shrub or small tree that typically grows in an upright, irregularly branched form to 10 to 20 feet tall and up to 10 feet wide. The leathery, glossy, evergreen, dark green leaves have toothed margins. Small greenish-white flowers appear on male and female plants in spring. Pollinated flowers on female plants give way to berry-like red fruits, which ripen in fall and persist into winter. USDA zones 7 to 10. Rain garden zone B.

Virginia sweetspire

Itea virginica
Virginia sweetspire

    USDA Zones 5 to 9

    Native

    3 to 5 feet tall, 3 to 8 feet wide

    Zone A, B

This erect, rounded, deciduous shrub has fragrant, tiny white flowers in drooping racemes that cover the shrub in early summer. The dark green leaves turn an attractive red in autumn, sometimes persisting on the shrub until December. Plants can form dense, unruly colonies by root suckering if left unchecked. Annual renewal pruning will help keep plants looking neat and in check.

Spicebush

Northern bayberry

Black chokeberry

Lindera benzoin

Spicebush

USDA Zones 4 to 9

Native

6 to 12 feet tall, 6 to 12 feet wide

Zone B

This deciduous shrub has a broad, rounded growth. Clusters of tiny, aromatic, greenish-yellow flowers bloom along the branches in early spring before the foliage emerges. Male and female flowers are on separate plants, with the male flowers being larger and showier than the female ones. Flowers of female plants give way to bright red drupes that mature in fall and are attractive to birds. Female plants need a male pollinator in order to set fruit. Thick, light green leaves turn an attractive yellow in autumn. Leaves are aromatic when crushed. Fall color is best in sunny areas. Plants tolerate full shade, but become more open and wide-spreading.

Myrica pensylvanica

Northern bayberry

USDA Zones 4 to 7

Native

3 to 8 feet tall

Zone B

Bayberry is a deciduous shrub with a rounded habit and leathery, glossy, grayish-green leaves that are aromatic when crushed. Flowers are not all that showy, but flowers on female plants, if pollinated, are followed by attractive clusters of tiny, grayish-white fruit in late summer that usually persist through the winter. This shrub prefers acidic soils but tolerates a wide range of soils and growing conditions, including drought, poor soils, wet soils, high winds, and salt spray. Groupings need at least one male plant to facilitate pollination of female plants and subsequent fruit set. Shrubs tend to sucker, and may form sizeable colonies in optimum growing conditions.

Other species: *M. cerifera* (southern bayberry) grows 8 to 20 feet tall and wide and can form large colonies. It is better suited to southeastern gardens. USDA zones 7 to 9. Rain garden zone B.

M. gale (sweet gale) is a suckering shrub growing 2 to 6 feet tall and wide. It is very hardy, from USDA zones 2 to 6. Rain garden zones A, B.

Photinia melanocarpa (Aronia melanocarpa)

Black chokeberry

USDA Zones 3 to 8

Native

3 to 6 feet tall, 3 to 6 feet wide

Zones A, B

This upright, mounded shrub has dark green, glossy summer foliage that turns a beautiful red in fall. White flowers produced in early May last for two weeks or more, then are followed by small black fruits. The lower branches often become sparse; hide them by using low-growing plants in front of black chokeberry. Plants do best if left untrimmed. This shrub can be somewhat invasive when the suckers are allowed to remain. Suckers are easily controlled with regular pruning if desired.

Cultivar: 'Autumn Magic' grows upright to 5 feet; it has good flower and fruit production and outstanding fall color.

Other species: P. *floribunda* (*A. arbutifolia*; red chokeberry) has bright red fruit and good reddish pink fall leaf color. It does sucker, but it can be shaped into a small tree with regular pruning. USDA zones 4 to 9. Rain garden zones A, B.

'Center Glow' ninebark

Physocarpus opulifolius
Common ninebark

> USDA Zones 3 to 8
> Native
> 5 to 8 feet tall
> Zone B

This tough and hardy multi-stemmed shrub produces fast-growing shoots that arch out and away from the center. The five-petaled, white to pinkish flowers are grouped together in 2-inch flat-topped clusters in June and July and are followed by somewhat showy reddish brown fruit. Older stems are covered with attractive shaggy bark that sloughs off in long fibrous strips, but the foliage usually covers it. The foliage stays clean and attractive throughout the growing season and can be shades of yellow or purple. Dried fruit can vary from brown to bright red, depending on soil and weather. Shape plants as needed by pruning immediately after flowering. Overgrown plants can be cut back in late winter but not every year.

Cultivars: Many cultivars are available and are usually better suited to landscape situations. 'Dart's Gold' grows to a compact 4 to 6 feet tall and wide with good foliage color. 'Diabolo' has distinctive purple foliage that ages to a bronze shade. It can be pruned harshly each spring to promote vigorous shoots with large, highly colored leaves. 'Nugget' grows to only 6 feet tall and wide and has greenish yellow, textured leaves. 'Snowfall' flowers more freely and has medium green leaves.

Other species: P. *capitatus* (Pacific ninebark) is an attractive western species better suited to Pacific Northwest rain gardens. It is hardy in USDA zones 4 to 8 and grows 3 to 8 feet tall. Rain garden zone B.

Arborvitae

Thuja occidentalis
Arborvitae

> USDA Zones 2 to 7
> Native
> 20 to 40 feet tall, 10 to 15 feet wide
> Zones A, B

This upright, pyramidal shrub or small tree is one of only a few evergreens well-suited to urban rain gardens. It has dense, scalelike, green to yellowish green foliage arranged in flat, fanlike branches. On mature trees the bark is gray to reddish brown, separating in long shreds, and the trunk is often twisted. Foliage and bark are aromatic. Foliage often looks slightly yellow, purple, or brown in winter but returns to green in summer. Plants provide excellent shelter for birds. Arborvitaes are slow-growing and long-lived. They are subject to winter burn, especially when planted on the south side of buildings; however, the winter burn is easy to prune out in spring because it occurs on outside leaves. Do not confuse winter burn with the normal browning of inside leaves as plants age or the normal color change arborvitaes go through in winter. Prune just after new growth has emerged. Deer are a serious problem, often completely defoliating the lower parts of trees.

Cultivars: Many cultivars have been selected for foliage color and growth habits. 'Hetz Midget' is a dense, globe-shaped selection that grows 2 feet tall and 3 feet wide. 'Holmstrup' is a tough, upright grower that stays under 8 feet tall. 'Techny' is a broad, pyramidal tree that is 25 feet tall and has good dark green color. 'Woodwardii' is a true globe, growing 5 to 6 feet tall and wide. USDA zones 3 to 6. Rain garden zone B.

Highbush blueberry

Vaccinium corymbosum
Highbush blueberry
> USDA Zones 3 to 8
> Native
> 3 to 10 feet tall, 3 to 10 feet wide
> Zones A, B ☀

This species is the parent of the many cultivated highbush blueberries grown for fruit. It is an upright, deciduous shrub with small, waxy, bell-shaped, white flowers that appear in spring. The berries appear in summer. The dark green leaves turn attractive shades of red and purple in fall. Birds love the fruit as much as people do. Yellow leaves may occur in soils with too high of a pH.

Other species: *V. angustifolium* (lowbush blueberry) stays under 2 feet tall and tolerates light shade. It makes a nice groundcover in rain garden zone C. USDA zones 3 to 7.

Arrowwood

Viburnum dentatum
Arrowwood
> USDA Zones 2 to 8
> Native
> 6 to 10 feet tall, 4 to 10 feet wide
> Zone A, B ☀ ☀

The white flowers of these easy-care, fast-growing deciduous shrubs appear in late spring, and plants have nice green summer foliage. Flowers give way to blue-black fruit that attracts birds and other wildlife. Variable fall color ranges from drab yellow to shades of orange and red to purple, depending on the species. Viburnums do not require a lot of pruning, but you can prune right after flowering to shape them or reduce their overall height. It is a good idea to remove a few of the older stems every three years or so to encourage new growth from the base. Prune immediately after flowering because flower buds form in summer for the following year.

Other species: *V. lentago* (nannyberry) is a 10- to 20-foot upright shrub or single-stemmed tree. It grows well in full sun to deep shade, but reddish purple fall color is best in sun. USDA zones 2 to 8. Rain garden zone B.

V. nudum (possum haw, withe-rod), an eastern species, grows 5 to 12 feet tall and has good fruit production and fall color. USDA zones 5 to 9. Rain garden zones A, B.

V. prunifolium (blackhaw) grows 12 to 15 feet tall and can be pruned as a small tree. USDA zones 3 to 9. Rain garden zone B.

V. rufidulum (rusty blackhaw), a southern species, typically grows 10 to 20 feet tall and wide. USDA zones 5 to 9. Rain garden zone B.

V. trilobum (highbush cranberry) grows 10 to 12 feet tall and wide. It has lovely, white, lace-cap flowers that grow up to 4 inches across, and the leaves turn beautiful shades of yellow-orange to red in fall. The showy, deep red fruit persists through winter. This plant prefers a slightly acidic soil in full sun to partial shade but will tolerate less-than-ideal situations. USDA zones 2 to 6. Rain garden zones A, B.

Other Shrubs and Small Trees to Consider, Listed with Their Rain Garden Zones

Beautyberry

Sweetshrub

Aesculus parviflora (bottlebrush buckeye)* B

Alnus species (alders)* A

Aralia spinosa (devil's walking stick)* B

Asimina triloba (pawpaw)* A, B

Callicarpa americana (beautyberry)* B

Calycanthus floridus (sweetshrub)* B, C

Chionanthus virginicus (white fringetree)* B

Corylus species (hazelnuts)* B

Diervilla species (bush honeysuckles)* B, C

Forsythia xintermedia (showy forsythia) B

Fothergilla species (fothergillas)* A, B

Gaylussacia species (huckleberries)* A, B

Holodiscus discolor (oceanspray)* B

Itea virginica (Virginia sweetspire)* A, B

Juniperus horizontalis (creeping juniper)* C

Juniperus virginiana (red cedar)* A, B

Kalmia species (mountain laurels)* A, B

Lonicera involucrata (twinberry)* B

Magnolia stellata (star magnolia) B

Magnolia xloebneri (magnolia) B

Mahonia aquifolium (Oregon grape)* C

Mahonia repens (creeping mahonia)* C

Morella californica (California wax myrtle)* C

Philadelphus lewesii (Lewis' mock orange)* B

Ptelea trifoliata (common hoptree)* B

Rhododendron arborescens (smooth azalea)* B

Rhododendron atlanticum (coast azalea)* B

Rhododendron canadense (rhodora)* A, B

Rhododendron maximum (rosebay, great laurel)* B

Creeping mahonia

Elderberry

Rhododendron periclymenoides (pinxterbloom azalea)* B

Rhododendron serrulatum (hammock-plain azalea)* A, B

Rhododendron viscosum (swamp azalea)* A, B

Rhus aromatica 'Gro-Low' (fragrant sumac)* B, C

Rhus copallinum (winged sumac)* B

Rhus glabra (smooth sumac)* B

Rhus typhina (staghorn sumac)* B

Ribes sanguineum (red-flowering currant)* B

Rosa nitida (shining rose)* B

Rosa palustris (swamp rose)* B

Rubus odoratus (purple-flowering raspberry)* B

Rubus parviflorus (thimbleberry)* B

Rubus spectabilis (salmonberry)* B

Sambucus species (elderberries)* A, B

Sassafras albidum (sassafras)* B

Spiraea alba (white meadowsweet)* A, B

Spiraea douglasii (rose spirea)* A, B

Spirea x bumalda 'Anthony Waterer' (Japanese spirea) B, C

Staphylea trifolia (American bladdernut)* B

Symphoricarpos albus (snowberry)* B, C

Syringa reticulata (Japanese tree lilac) B

*North American natives

Trees

Red maple

Acer rubrum

Red maple

    USDA Zones 3 to 9

    Native

    40 to 65 feet tall

    Zones A, B

Red maple is a medium-sized tree with a broadly rounded symmetrical crown. Leaves have three- to five-pointed, saw-toothed lobes. Fall color is usually a brilliant red, but it can also be orange or yellow. The small red flowers give the bare branches a red glow for a week or so in early to mid-April, before the leaves appear. This tree prefers slightly acidic soil and will not grow well on alkaline soils. Otherwise it is tolerant of urban conditions. It has a wide native range; stick with local seed strains and sources for best results.

Other species: *A. circinatum* (vine maple) is a western species well suited to rain gardens in the Pacific Northwest. It is a small tree or large shrub, growing only 15 to 25 feet tall. It prefers partial shade. USDA zones 6 to 9. Rain garden zone B.

    A. saccharum (sugar maple) grows 50 to 80 feet tall and has brilliant fall color ranging from yellow to orange to scarlet. It is sensitive to salt damage, so avoid using it as a street tree. USDA zones 3 to 8. Rain garden zone B.

River birch

Hackberry

Black gum

Betula nigra
River birch

> USDA Zones 4 to 9
> Native
> 40 to 70 feet tall
> Zones A, B

River birch can be grown as a single- or multi-trunked tree. The distinctive bark is highly ornamental; it is shiny and varies in color from red-brown to cinnamon-brown with a touch of salmon pink. It peels off in large horizontal strips. On older trees, the bark is darker and corkier. Fall color is yellow to green and is not as ornamental as other birches. This tree needs a soil pH below 6.5; acidify soil before planting, if needed. The brittle, twiggy branches break easily in windstorms, and catkins dropping in late spring can be messy, but only for a short period. River birch is highly resistant to bronze birch borer and is rarely troubled by leaf miners.

Celtis occidentalis
Hackberry

> USDA Zones 2 to 9
> Native
> 40 to 70 feet tall
> Zones A, B

Hackberry's form varies from a vase-shaped, upright tree to one with an open, wide-spreading crown. Fall color is yellow to greenish yellow. The small fruit turns from orange-red to purple and often hangs on for much of the winter. Mature trees have interesting deep, corky bark with warty protrusions. This tree's adaptability to a wide range of conditions makes hackberry good for street use. It can tolerate wind, full sun, and the dirt and grime of city conditions; the rough bark offers protection along city streets. Hackberry is among the best food and shelter trees for wildlife. Birds and mammals eat the fruits, and leaves are the larval food of many butterflies. The narrow limb crotches and numerous spur branches attract many nesting birds. Hackberry transplants easily but sometimes takes up to two years to really start growing after planting. After that, it is moderately fast-growing. A few cosmetic problems affect hackberry, but none of them are serious. Hackberry nipple gall is a wartlike growth on the lower side of leaves caused by insects known as psyllids. Clusters of twiggy outgrowth called witches' brooms appear on some branches, caused by feeding mites and a powdery mildew fungus.

Nyssa sylvatica
Black gum

> USDA Zones 5 to 9
> Native
> 30 to 60 feet tall
> Zones A, B

Black gum has a distinctive silhouette, often with drooping branches that are very crooked toward their ends. Leaves are shiny green in summer, turning an amazing yellow to orange to scarlet to purple in fall. Insignificant flowers in spring turn into bluish black fruit in fall. It is not a good choice for a street tree because it is intolerant of pollution. The flowers are attractive to bees, and the fruit is eaten by wildlife. It likes slightly acidic soil; trees will develop iron chlorosis (yellow leaves) if the soil is too alkaline. You may need to top dress soil with acidic fertilizer to maintain the necessary soil pH. Cankers may develop causing branches to die back. Remove infected branches. Keep pruning to a minimum to emphasis the natural shape.

Swamp white oak

Quercus bicolor
Swamp white oak
>   USDA Zones 3 to 8
>   Native
>   50 to 60 feet tall
>   Zones A, B

Swamp white oak has an open, rounded crown and makes a handsome specimen or shade tree. It is faster growing and more tolerant of tough sites than most oaks, but it does best on a slightly acidic soil. Fall leaf color is an attractive bronze-brown. Oak roots are very sensitive to changes in soil level. Even a small change can kill roots, so avoid adding or removing soil around trees. Oak wilt, a fungal disease, can kill mature oaks; red oaks are more susceptible than white oaks. The oak wilt fungus enters trees via insects through wounds caused by pruning, or by root damage during construction. The fungus can spread to nearby trees by root grafts. Oak wilt is mainly a problem on native stands; usually landscape specimens are isolated enough not to be at risk. Do not prune oaks while insects are most active, from April 1 to July 1.

Other Species: *Q. palustris* (pin oak) is relatively fast growing and easy to transplant, making it a good choice for landscape use. It requires acidic soil. USDA zones 4 to 8. Rain garden zones A, B.

Most other species of oak will do fine in rain garden zone B if you have the room for them.

Bald cypress

Taxodium distichum
Bald cypress
>   USDA Zones 5 to 10
>   Native
>   60 to 90 feet tall
>   Zone A

Bald cypress is a long-lived, pyramidal conifer that looks like a needled evergreen, but it is deciduous, losing its leaves in winter. The soft, feathery, yellowish-green needles turn an attractive orange/cinnamon-brown in fall and the purplish-green cones mature to brown. It withstands urban conditions quite well but requires an acidic soil; needle yellowing will occur on alkaline soils. Trees grown in drier soils do not develop the distinct "knees" that those grown in swamps do.

Sweet gum

Other Trees to Consider, listed with their Rain Garden Zones

Aesculus flava (yellow buckeye)* B

Carya glabra (pignut hickory)* B

Carya ovata (shagbark hickory)* B

Chamaecyparis thyoides (Atlantic white cedar)* A

Cladrastis kentukea (Kentucky yellowwood)* B

Ginkgo biloba (ginkgo) B

Gymnocladus dioicus (Kentucky coffeetree)* B

Larix laricina (tamarack)* A

Liquidambar styraciflua (sweet gum)* B

Magnolia tripetala (umbrella-tree)* B

Magnolia virginiana (sweetbay)* A, B

*North American natives

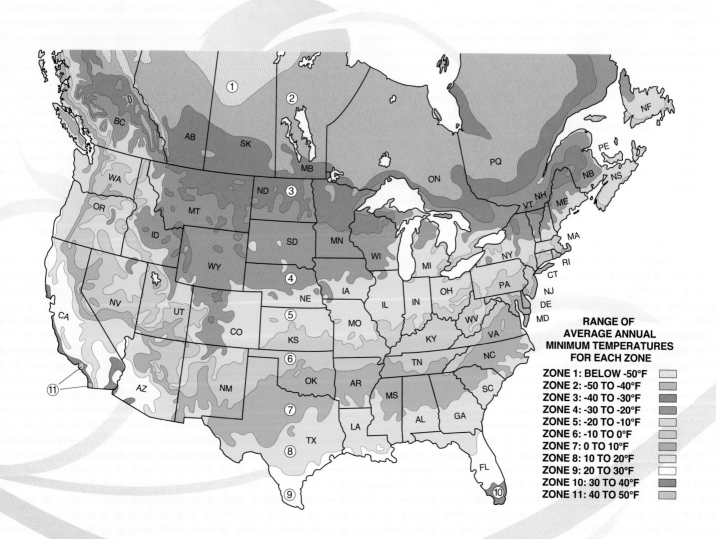

RANGE OF AVERAGE ANNUAL MINIMUM TEMPERATURES FOR EACH ZONE

ZONE 1: BELOW -50°F
ZONE 2: -50 TO -40°F
ZONE 3: -40 TO -30°F
ZONE 4: -30 TO -20°F
ZONE 5: -20 TO -10°F
ZONE 6: -10 TO 0°F
ZONE 7: 0 TO 10°F
ZONE 8: 10 TO 20°F
ZONE 9: 20 TO 30°F
ZONE 10: 30 TO 40°F
ZONE 11: 40 TO 50°F

RESOURCES

Rain Garden Information

Blue Thumb Guide to Raingardens, Rusty Schmidt, Dan Shaw, and David Dods, 2007. Waterdrop Innovations. www.bluethumb.org/raingardens.

California Sea Grant, University of California, San Diego. www-csgc.ucsd.edu/BOOKSTORE/Resources.

Geauga Soil and Water Conservation District (Northeast Ohio). www.cuyahogaswcd.org/PDFs/RainGardenManual.pdf.

North Carolina Cooperative Extension. www.bae.ncsu.edu/topic/raingarden.

Rain Garden Design and Construction Northern Virginia Homeowners Guide. www.fairfaxcounty.gov/nvswcd/raingardenbk.pdf.

Rain Gardens: A How-to Manual for Homeowners, WI Dept. Natural Resources and UW-Extension Publication, 2003. University of Wisconsin Extension. http://learningstore.uwex.edu/assets/pdfs/GWQ037.pdf.

Washington State University Extension (nice video on rain gardens). http://raingarden.wsu.edu/HomeownerResources.html.

Native Plants Information

Cullina, William. 2000. *Guide to Growing and Propagating Wildflowers of the United States and Canada*. New York: Houghton Mifflin.

Cullina, William. 2002. *Native Trees, Shrubs, and Vines: A Guide to Using, Growing, and Propagating North American Woody Plants*. New York: Houghton Mifflin.

Cullina, William. 2008. *Native Ferns, Moss & Grasses*. New York: Houghton Mifflin.

Illinois Wildflowers. www.illinoiswildflowers.info/index.htm.

Kemper Center for Home Gardening PlantFinder, Missouri Botanical Garden. www.mobot.org/gardeninghelp/plantinfo.shtml.

Lady Bird Johnson Wildflower Center. www.wildflower.org/explore.

Missouri Botanical Garden Kemper Center for Home Gardening. www.mobot.org/gardinghelp/plantfinder/Alpha.asp.

Prairie Moon Nursery, Upper Midwest Native plants and seeds. www.prairiemoon.com.

Steiner, Lynn M. 2006. *Landscaping with Native Plants of Michigan*. St. Paul, Minnesota: Voyageur Press.

Steiner, Lynn M. 2005. *Landscaping with Native Plants of Minnesota*. Stillwater, Minnesota: Voyageur Press.

Steiner, Lynn M. 2007. *Landscaping with Native Plants of Wisconsin*. St. Paul, Minnesota: Voyageur Press.

Tallamy, Douglas W. 2007. *Bringing Nature Home: How Native Plants Sustain Wildlife in Our Gardens*. Portland, Oregon: Timber Press.

USDA Plants Database. http://plants.usda.gov.

Index

Index

ABOUT THE AUTHORS

Lynn Steiner has a master's degree in horticulture and is one of the Upper Midwest's best-known gardening writers. The author of three *Landscaping with Native Plants* books and the former editor of *Northern Gardener* magazine, she is a frequent speaker at gardening and environmental events. Steiner lives in Stillwater, Minnesota.

Robert Domm is a scientist with the Water Resources Group of Tetra Tech, Inc., where he specializes in stormwater best management practices. As a photographer, his work has appeared in numerous publications, including magazines, textbooks, and calendars. Author of several books, including *Michigan Yesterday & Today* and *Lake Michigan Backroads*, Domm lives in Rives Junction, Michigan.

ACKNOWLEDGMENTS

Our heartfelt thanks are owed to many people who helped make this book possible.

For allowing us to visit and photograph their beautiful gardens, homes, and places of business, we would like to thank Gary Britton, Paul and Susan Damon, Deb Ferrington, Diane Hilscher, Mary Kearney, Howard and Frances Knorr, Maplewood City Hall, Jeremy Mayberg and Amy-Ann Greenspan, Mequon Unitarian Church, Robert and Marlene Olsen, Kent Peterson, Veronika Phillips, Linda Piotrowski, Connie Ramthun, Kadi Renowden, Bill Schneider of Wildtype Nursery, Fred and Marcy Schramm, Connie and Ken Taillon, Andy and Carolyn Van Sickle, Amy Welsh, and Barb Wolter. Special thanks to Anne and Eric Thomas who graciously allowed Robert to photograph the installation of their rain garden.

Thanks to Connie Taillon, Ward Wilson, and Diane Denning for allowing us to use their photographs in the book. Thanks to Jeff Domm and Simeon Cochrane for their great illustrations.

For their help in locating gardens to photograph, Lynn would like to thank Eric Olsen of Outback Nursery; Diane Hilscher of Hilscher Design and Ecology; Mike Evenocheck of Prairie Restorations, Inc.; and Marty Rice of Wild Ones.

Thanks to Anne Thomas, P. E. and Dan Christian, P. E. for sharing their expertise and for their technical proofreading.

Our appreciation goes to the scientific and natural areas in Wisconsin and Minnesota where Lynn was able to enjoy, study, and photograph native plants, as well as these public gardens: Birmingham Botanical Garden, Cornell Plantation Garden, Minnesota Landscape Arboretum, Missouri Botanical Garden, and Shaw Nature Reserve.

First published in 2012 by Voyageur Press, an imprint of MBI Publishing Company, 400 First Avenue North, Suite 300, Minneapolis, MN 55401 USA

Voyageur Press titles are also available at discounts in bulk quantity for industrial or sales-promotional use. For details write to Special Sales Manager at MBI Publishing Company, 400 First Avenue North, Suite 300, Minneapolis, MN 55401 USA.

To find out more about our books, visit us online at www.voyageurpress.com.

Library of Congress Cataloging-in-Publication Data

Steiner, Lynn M., 1958-
Rain gardens : sustainable landscaping for a beautiful yard and a healthy world / Lynn M. Steiner and Robert W. Domm. -- 1st ed.
    p. cm.
Includes index.
ISBN 978-0-7603-4044-8 (softbound)
1. Rain gardens. 2. Runoff--Management. 3. Ecological landscape design. I. Domm, Robert W. II. Title. III. Title: Sustainable landscaping for a beautiful yard and a healthy world.
TD657.4.S74 2012
635.9'5--dc23
                    2011024587

1 2 3 4 5 6

Editor: Melinda Keefe
Design Manager: Cindy Samargia Laun
Designed by: Karl Laun

Cover photo: © Paul Markert
Summersweet photo pg. 175: © Missouri Botanical Garden PlantFinder/Glenn Kopp
Virginia sweetspire photo pg. 178: © Payless Images/Shutterstock.com
Spicebush photo pg. 179: © Missouri Botanical Garden PlantFinder/Thomas Pope
Northern Bayberry photo pg. 179: © Missouri Botanical Garden PlantFinder/Chris Starbuck
Highbush blueberry photo pg. 181: © jadimages/Shutterstock.com
Bald cypress photo pg. 185: © Ihervas/Dreamstime.com

Printed in China